Se

Ancient
World

Secrets of the
Ancient
World

Exploring the Insights of America's Most Well-Documented Psychic, Edgar Cayce

**Lora H. Little, Ed.D.
Gregory L. Little, Ed.D.
John Van Auken**

ARE
PRESS

ASSOCIATION FOR
RESEARCH AND
ENLIGHTENMENT

A.R.E. Press • Virginia Beach • Virginia

A.R.E. Press
215 67th Street
Virginia Beach, VA 23451–2061

Library of Congress Cataloguing–in–Publication Data
Little, Lora H.
    Secrets of the ancient world : exploring the insights of America's most well–documented psychic, Edgar Cayce / by Lora H. Little, Gregory L. Little, and John Van Auken.
        p.   cm.
    ISBN 0–87604–481–X (pbk.)
    1. Parapsychology and archaeology.   2. Antiquities–Miscellanea. 3. Bible–Miscellanea.   4. Cayce, Edgar, 1877–1945. Edgar Cayce readings.   I. Little, Gregory L.   II. Van Auken, John.   III. Title.
BF1045.A74L58 2003
133.8'092—dc22

                                          2003019972

Cover design by Richard Boyle

Contents

1

Introduction

For, what the entity is today is the result of what it has been in days and experiences and ages and eons past. For, life is continuous; and whether it is manifested in materiality or in the realm of an individuality alone, it is one and the same. And it is brought into being that it might be one with its Maker.   2051-5

For that which is *was* and ever will be. Only the mortal or material, or matter, changeth; but the expressions of same prompted by the Spirit of truth live on.   1448-2

O, ye say, this is not new! Neither is thy present disturbance, nor thy present hope, nor *anything!* For, even as he said, "There is nothing new under the sun." What is has been, and will be again.   3976-27

Edgar Cayce's readings include a fascinating story of the *millions of years of human history.* In this book, many aspects of that story are summarized and expanded upon in light of the latest scientific and historical discoveries. Most of the chapters are updates of articles originally written for the newsletter *Ancient Mysteries,* published monthly by the Association for Research and Enlightenment (A.R.E.). However, the original information has been supplemented to reflect the wealth of archaeological and genetic evidence being uncovered almost daily.

Writing this book was especially exciting because, since 1997, a great deal of groundbreaking data has emerged to confirm much of the heretofore unknown and very detailed historical accounts contained within the Cayce readings. What was once considered to be incredible and impossible now appears to be both credible and probable. It is an astonishing turn of events. For this reason, we feel that it is important to make Cayce's information on ancient events more widely available.

Also, since the readings continually emphasized that we are often unconsciously repeating dysfunctional patterns that have manifested throughout the history of man, we desperately need to understand our past. By studying and learning from our history, perhaps we can change our future for the better.

Edgar Cayce—from the Edgar Cayce Foundation.

The Headquarters of the Association for Research and Enlightenment (A.R.E.) in Virginia Beach, Virginia—from the Edgar Cayce Foundation.

WHO WAS EDGAR CAYCE?

Many of our readers are familiar with Edgar Cayce, the man many call "America's greatest psychic." He was born in 1877 near Hopkinsville, Kentucky, and died in 1945 in Virginia Beach, Virginia. Although he was brought up in a fundamentalist Christian environment, he began having unusual experiences of a paranormal nature in early childhood. His mother, upon becoming aware of his strange abilities, assured him that it must be a gift from God and should only be used to help others. She especially insisted that it not be used to show off or to take advantage of others.

For the most part, Cayce lived up to these ideals. Living close to poverty most of his life, he received very little monetary benefit from his gifts and often suffered ridicule. Despite the limited material rewards, while reclining in a sleeplike state he gave over 14,000 psychic readings to individuals from all walks of life. These readings were carefully documented and catalogued and are available to the public at the headquarters of the A.R.E., which Cayce founded in 1931 in Virginia Beach, Virginia. They are also available to members of the association through the A.R.E. web site (www.edgarcayce.org).

The fact that nearly everything Cayce said during his psychic trances was recorded in writing is notable and distinguishes him from countless others who have claimed psychic ability. Because of this, the Cayce readings can be tested for accuracy, and many people have done so. The A.R.E. has encouraged such research by making the Cayce readings available on a searchable computer CD-ROM. Articles and books reporting on Cayce's accuracy all tend to show that his information was between 80 and 90 percent accurate—an astonishing percentage.

WHAT THE READINGS CONTAIN

Most of Cayce's readings were health-related. For various disorders, he recommended a host of remedies, most of which remain in use today. As a result, Cayce is generally acknowledged to be the father of the contemporary "holistic heath" movement in America. He was closely studied by many famous physicians of his day because of his unusual ability to diagnose illness without having to be in the same room with the patient. Despite the fact that the waking Cayce had a very limited education, when giving a reading he was able to successfully describe and recommend a treatment for medical problems that even today are considered incurable. When asked in a reading how this ability worked, he indicated that while in the "sleeping" state, he was able to access the deeper mind of the patient and a universal spiritual source he called the Akashic record. His medical readings are so comprehensive and unusual that they continue to be the focus of research by professionals in the fields of medicine and psychology, as well as by organizations such as the Meridian Institute in Virginia Beach.

But health was not the only topic that emerged in the readings. To his initial horror as a devout Christian, Cayce's readings also covered information related to reincarnation. In 1923 in Dayton, Ohio, a man named Arthur Lammers asked the sleeping Cayce a set of philosophical questions that went beyond just physical health. During this series of questions, Cayce began to talk about reincarnation as if it were as real and natural as the functioning of the physical body. This shocked and challenged Cayce and his family. They were deeply religious people, doing this work to help others simply because that's what their Christian faith taught. As a child, Cayce had read the Bible from front to back, and continued this practice until he had read it through once for every year of his life. Reincarnation was not part of the Cayce family's reality. Yet, the healings and the help for others continued.

Over time, the readings began to reveal that some physical illnesses were related to the past lives of the patients. Ultimately, the Cayce family began to accept this strange idea, although not as "reincarnation" per se. Edgar Cayce preferred to call it "the continuity of life." He felt that the Bible did contain much evidence that life—the true life in the Spirit— is continual.

In September 1925, Cayce moved his family to Virginia Beach, Virginia, where he set up a hospital and continued to give health readings. In addition, he began giving what are called "life readings" for individuals who wanted to know about their previous lives. From 1925 through 1944, he conducted some 2,500 life readings, describing the past lives of individuals as casually as if everyone understood reincarnation to be a reality.[1] Such subjects as deep-seated fears, mental blocks, vocational talents, innate urges and abilities, marriage difficulties, and child training were examined in the light of what the readings called "karmic patterns" resulting from previous lives.

CAYCE'S STORY OF THE HISTORY OF HUMANITY

In the one before this we find in that fair country of Alta, or Poseidia proper, when this entity was in that force that brought the highest civilization and knowledge that has been known to the earth's plane . . . This we find nearly ten thousand years before the Prince of Peace [*Christ*] came . . .

288-1

The sleeping Edgar Cayce spoke these words on November 20, 1923, while giving a life reading for an eighteen-year-old female. In place of her name, she was assigned the number "288" for confidentiality. The number "1" after the hyphen above indicates this was her first reading.

This particular reading is significant because it was the first of 672 life readings that described a highly advanced civilization existing prior to recorded history. In fact, Atlantis was mentioned in about 27 percent of the 2500 total life readings given by Cayce.[2] What is especially intriguing about these readings is their consistency when readings for different individuals are compared. Many of the Atlantis-related readings were given decades apart, and yet they picked up the story in such a way that they remained true to a coherent account of the very distant past. For example, three major environmental catastrophes were repeatedly referred to as occurring about 10,000 B.C., 28,000 B.C., and 50,000 B.C. Most shocking of all was the readings' assertion that not only had Atlantis come into being around 200,000 B.C.,[3] but it had been preceded by another civilization called Lemuria, or Mu, in which primitive, humanlike life had begun over ten million years ago![4] What was revealed about these mysterious civilizations was so compelling that readings were requested specifically to explore them, ultimately leading to additional information that outlined the history of humanity as far back as Creation.

Edgar Cayce was not the first to mention the existence of Lemuria and Atlantis. James Churchward wrote several books in the early twentieth century relating his research in India where ancient records were said to contain references to Lemuria.[5] Plato told of Atlantis circa (ca.) 340 B.C. in two of his works, *Timaeus* and *Critias*. He claimed that his information was received from his grandfather, Critias, who received it from Solon, an Athenian statesman. Solon had visited with a group of Egyptian priests who were guardians of secret information concerning an advanced island civilization that existed "beyond the gates of Hercules" and had been destroyed around 9600 B.C. Plato's writings contain an astonishing abundance of detail including the architecture, city layout, and culture of the people.

The lost civilization of Atlantis appears to have been treated mostly as fable by Plato's peers, including Aristotle. It was later picked up in the first century A.D. by Pliny, a Roman historian, in his encyclopedic book, *Natural History*. In 1627, Frances Bacon used Plato's story in his book, *The New Atlantis*, which was an attempt to describe a model civilization based on an appreciation for science and the arts. The possibility of Atlantis' existence was the subject of much debate by great thinkers such as Voltaire, Montaigne, and Buffon. Since the late nineteenth century, thousands of books and articles have been written about Atlantis. Ignatius Donnelly's *Atlantis: The Antediluvian World* is considered the most thorough and best known. Recent books, such as Graham Hancock's *Fingerprints of the Gods*[6] and *Underworld*[7], Andrew Collins's *Gateway to Atlantis*[8] and *From the Ashes of Angels*[9], as well as our own *Lost Hall of Records*[10], *Mound Builders*[11], and *Ancient South America*[12], have presented evidence for the existence of a pre-Ice Age civilization from a scientific viewpoint. However, despite mounting evidence to the contrary, Atlantis is still considered by many in America's scientific circles to be nothing more than a myth.

The Cayce readings not only addressed civilizations of prehistory, but also gave us a unique insight into the life and times of people living during the era covered in biblical history. An avid reader of the Bible and a popular Sunday School teacher in his waking life, Cayce was gratified to find that some people's past lives had occurred within the context of some of his favorite Scripture stories. When pieced together into a whole, these readings provide information that greatly deepens and expands our understanding of the lives of the Patriarchs of the Bible and, most particularly, the life of Jesus. It is often said that the Cayce readings make the Bible come to life.[13] In addition, the accuracy of some parts of these readings, which seemed unlikely according to the known biblical archaeology of Cayce's lifetime, have now been verified.

For example, there are many readings that refer to a pre–Christian Hebrew group called the Essenes, whose existence was not confirmed until the discovery of the Dead Sea Scrolls shortly after Cayce's death.

HOW THIS BOOK IS ORGANIZED

This collection of separately written articles has here been arranged as a series of chapters in roughly historically chronological order:

- The book begins with chapters that summarize Cayce's story of Creation and the lives of important characters that the readings tell us lived in Atlantis. These chapters provide background information to support later ones.

- Following these chapters is a cutting–edge discussion of the latest discoveries in the field of genetics and how this evidence has dramatically changed the mainstream view of the origins of various ancient cultures. In addition, it summarizes how this new view supports much of Cayce's story.

- Most of the chapters that follow highlight a particular culture, period of history, or geographical setting and discuss the ancient mysteries associated with them. This group includes a chapter that reviews the ongoing search for the Atlantean Halls of Records that Cayce said could be found in Egypt, the Yucatan, and near Bimini.

- The final three chapters deal with some of Cayce's prophetic material concerning the second coming of Christ, possible future earth changes, and a major shift in human consciousness predicted to begin within our lifetime.

Each chapter includes not only the stories and ideas as they evolve in the readings, but also parallel ideas from ancient texts, historical research, and recent relevant scientific research. References to such resources and to Cayce readings are keyed to numbers in the text and are listed by chapter at the back of the book.

This book is not meant to be a comprehensive review of all of the ancient mysteries material available in the Cayce readings, but is a significant sampling of the many fascinating accounts that add so much to our understanding of ourselves and our history as human beings.

2

Origin of the Races: Oneness in Diversity

(. . . as man appearing from those projections in the five places—and, as has been given, from their environ took on that as became necessary for the meeting of those varying conditions under which their individualities and personalities began to put on form)—one in the white, another in the brown, another in the black, another in the red.   364-9

For know that *God* is not a respecter of persons nor of races, but is as has been given of old, "Know the Lord thy God is *One!*" And if the activities are for an active service in that direction, prejudices are lost sight of in the Love Divine.   1438-1

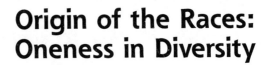

The Bible tells us that we are all descended from Noah, who was in turn descended from Seth, a son of the first couple, Adam and Eve. Traditional biblical chronology traces this first couple back to about 4004 B.C. Sometime later, Noah's three sons are assumed to have differentiated into the various races of man we know today. However, recent genetic studies indicate that the ancestry of all currently living human beings can be traced back to a single woman.[1] Dubbed "Mitochondrial Eve" (ME), this woman supposedly lived in Africa about 200,000 years ago. In addition, archaeologists have found evidence that human, hominid–type ancestors roamed the earth as long as eight million years ago.[2] Does this mean that biblical history as outlined in the book of Genesis is merely allegorical? And if mankind can be traced back to the same mother, why are we divided into such seemingly dissimilar groups or races? In addition, with whom did this first woman mate?

Scientists have several, mostly conflicting theories, including the discovery of "Y Chromosomal Adam," who appears to have originated several thousand years *later* than his female counterpart, ME.[3] To further complicate matters, recent analysis of ancient DNA obtained from 68,000–year–old Australian bones yielded no linkage whatsoever to ME. Fortunately for us, the history of humanity as outlined by the Edgar Cayce readings is not only able to account for the biblical story, but may even clarify what seems to be incompatible scientific evidence. But to explain the differences in (and the oneness of) the races of humanity, we must start at the beginning of creation.

In the Beginning: What the Bible Tells Us

Most Bible scholars agree that Genesis provides us with two different creation stories. The first, with which the Bible begins, tells of the creation of the world in six days by a plural God who the Hebrews call the Elohim. "In the beginning God created the heaven and the earth. And the Spirit of God moved upon the face of the waters. And God said, Let there be light; and there was light . . . " (Gen. 1:1, 3–4) On the sixth day of this first creation story, man is created: "And God said, let us make man in our image after our likeness . . . So God created man in his own image, in the image of God he created them; male and female created he them." (Gen. 1:26–27)

The second creation story begins with Chapter 2 of Genesis and tells the familiar story of Adam and Eve in the Garden of Eden. In this version, Adam is "formed of the dust of the ground," not by a plural God as in the previous creation story, but by an individualized "Lord God." (Gen. 2:7)

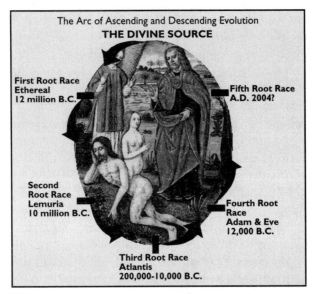

The arc of ascending and descending evolution
—by G. Little.

THE ARC OF ASCENDING AND DESCENDING EVOLUTION

According to the Cayce readings, these seemingly conflicting stories are included in the Bible for a reason. They form a highly condensed version of the full story of creation, which began many billions of years ago and is still playing out. The readings describe an arc of spiritual and physical devolution followed by a future evolutionary return to a state of oneness with the Father.[5] As the readings put it: " . . . all vibration must eventually, as it materializes into matter, pass through a stage of evolution and out. For it rises in its emanations and descends also. Hence the cycle, or circle, or arc, that is as a description of all influence in the experience of man."[6]

Throughout this arc, there have been key turning points that have involved changes in the spiritual and physical bodies of the human race. In theosophy, these points are referred to as the "seven root races," which W. H. Church[7] believes correspond to Cayce's "seven stages of man's development."[8] The term *root race* is actually mentioned in only two readings.[9] In one of those readings, we are told that the next evolutionary step for humanity—the fifth root race—will coincide with the future opening of the Atlantean Halls of Records. Cayce states that the Halls " . . . may not be entered without an understanding, for those that were left as guards may *not* be passed until after a period of their regeneration in the Mount, or the fifth root race begins."[10] The readings further indicate that this opening, and thus the entrance of the next root race, may be imminent![11]

CAYCE ON MULTIPLE CREATIONS AND ROOT RACES

According to the readings, then, the first biblical creation story refers to an initial creation of mankind as spiritual, free-will companions to the Father. At this point, man was an androgynous spiritual being ("male and female he created them") in full communication and oneness with the Creator. Sometime later, many of the entities began to get curious about the workings of the rest of creation. They then used their free will to project themselves into the denser world of matter.[12] This turning point is what Church[13] and Van Auken and Little[14] call Cayce's *first root race.*

Originally, the idea was to observe and learn, but eventually these very fluid and ethereal beings decided to draw closer into material form by creating and occupying humanoid life forms of a lower vibration. This was the *second root race.* At this point, they were still androgynous and could move in and out of their earthly bodies. They began to form communities on earth, and many resided in the land masses centering around the Pacific Ocean, which Cayce called Mu or Lemuria. One individual was told in a reading that her cave drawings, made ten million years ago in Lemuria, could still be found in the American Southwest.[15]

Over millions of years, this group became increasingly focused into their earthly creations until they lost even more of their connection with the Creator. They could no longer come and go into matter at will. Still androgynous, they retained some of their spiritual powers and were able to live thousands of years. However, they were using their abilities primarily for selfish reasons. One of the worst examples was their creation of "things" to serve as slaves. These creatures were materialized thought projections in the form of animal-human or plant-human hybrids. This period coincides with the origins of Atlantis, about 200,000

B.C., and is considered to be the *third root race*.[16]

As a result of this continued devolution, the Christ Spirit developed a plan to rescue these souls so that they could regain their rightful spiritual heritage. About 106,000 B.C., Amilius, the Atlantean Christ incarnation, and a group of other spiritual beings incarnated into Atlantis, where they too eventually became enmeshed in matter.[17] Amilius was one of the first to separate into two sexes, when his female half projected out as Lilith (discussed in more detail in the next chapter). Sometime later, Amilius determined that a new physical body would need to be developed for mankind in order for evolution out of the earth plane to occur. The physical form of an earlier Atlantean incarnation of Edgar Cayce (about 50,000 B.C.) was one of the forerunners of this new body.[18] However, the final perfected version—the *fourth root race*—was not unveiled until about 12,000 B.C.[19]

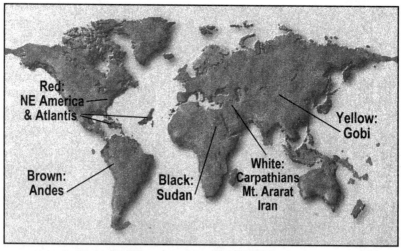

Map of the world ca. 12,000 B.C. per Edgar Cayce with locations of the first appearance of each of the five races of the fourth root race—by G. Little.

THE FOURTH ROOT RACE AND THE FIVE ADAMS AND EVES

This is where we first encounter Cayce's story of the origin of the races as we know them today. This is also the evolutionary stage he identifies with the second creation story in Genesis.[20] Once the fourth-root-race body was ready, the Christ Spirit incarnated as Adam and Eve in five different races and in five separate areas on the earth *simultaneously*: The red race incarnated in Atlantis (and North America) among the racially chameleon-like, third-root-race Atlanteans. The white race incarnated near Mt. Ararat, in the Carpathians, and in Iran. The other three races incarnated in the Gobi area of China (yellow), in the African Sudan and Egypt (black), and in the Andes area of South America (brown).[21]

Interestingly, Cayce emphasized that skin color was not the important differentiation for these five groups: "For He hath made of one blood the nations of the earth."[22] Instead, he asserted that the colors actually symbolized an inner law or thought pattern which involved one of the five senses. The yellow race he described as "mingling in the hearing," while the white and red were specifically connected to vision/sight and feeling/touch, respectively.[23] The black and brown races were not so clearly identified with a specific sense, but some Cayce scholars, such as Church, have interpreted the readings as assigning sense of taste to the black race and sense of smell to the brown race.[24] Souls could incarnate into each of the races in order to focus on the spiritual issues associated with the corresponding sense.

THE ONENESS OF ALL RACES

Cayce indicated that there has been much intermixing since the projection of these five races. Also, he seems to reinforce a recent scientific finding regarding the importance of environment in influencing the amount of the color-producing pigment, melanin, present in the skin. "For they are all one; there's no races, they are all one—they either have enjoined or have separated themselves, and as has been indicated from times back the environmental influences have made for changes in the color, or the food or the activity has produced those various things . . . "[25]

"Would snow be the place for the black? Or the sun the place for the white? Or the desert and the hills for either the white or black? As were partakers of those things that brought about those variations in that which enters, or becomes as the outer presentation, or the skin, or the pigment that is presented in same." [26]

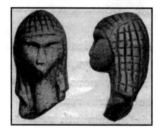

Stone age female goddess statues found throughout Europe ca. 30,000 B.C.—from: Boule, M., *Les Hommes Fossiles* (1923).

WAS MITOCHONDRIAL EVE AN ATLANTEAN?

Since ME is believed to have lived about 200,000 B.C., could she perhaps have been one of the androgynous Atlanteans—even the unseparated Amilius/Lilith-soul? According to the readings, the feminine side was often dominant, which could have caused the projected earthly body to contain only female characteristics.[27] If so, this may explain why Y Chromosomal Adam appears later in our genetic heritage, since in Cayce's story the split into separate sexes occurred sometime later. And what about the 60,000–year-old Australian DNA that could not be linked with ME? Cayce indicates that even as each new root race was developing, the previous one did not immediately die out. Scientists have seen this very pattern in the co-existence of Neanderthal Man and Cro-Magnon Man.

SCIENCE AND THE FIRST HUMAN APPEARANCE ON EARTH

The readings were adamant that " . . . Man did not descend from the monkey, but man has evolved, resuscitation, you see, from time to time . . . " resulting in ever-developing root races.[28] However, in 1925, Edgar Cayce made a rather startling statement regarding the appearance of physical, humanlike life on earth: Souls began to incarnate on earth over ten million years ago![29] Other readings implied that these first life forms with souls were primitive and had quite limited consciousness.[30] Interestingly, in 1925, scientists believed that humanlike creatures had not been around even one million years. For example, the 1922 text-book *The Outline of Science* placed the appearance of upright-walking hominids at approximately 500,000 years ago. The first primates were placed at only 1.2 million years ago.

A mid-July 2002 issue of the journal *Nature* reported that the oldest known skull of a hominid (our earliest ancestral relative) had been found in Chad (Africa) by a forty-member research team, led by French pale-ontologist Michel Brunet. It has been dated to between seven and eight million years old. Bernard Wood, a George Washington University pa-leontologist, stated that a poorly understood group of upright-walking hominids was "knocking around between five and eight million years ago for which there's a very poor fossil record." He termed the find "the tip of the iceberg—one that could sink our current ideas about evolution."

In 2001, two additional finds in Africa were reported. In February 2001, French paleontologists discovered a six-million-year-old hominid species in Kenya.[31] In July 2001, paleontologists discovered hominid re-mains in Ethiopia that dated to nearly six million years ago.[32] The result of these finds is another astounding near-confirmation of the "impos-sible dates" Cayce gave in the 1920s. Scientists will no doubt make fur-ther discoveries ever approaching Cayce's date (ten million years ago) for humanity's appearance on earth.

One aspect of this research may confuse those who are familiar with the Cayce readings that place the earliest appearance of humanity in

Artist's reconstruction of an early hominid man—from *The Outline of Science* **(1922).**

Mu and southwest America. Recall, however, that the readings also relate that the majority of the ancient continent Mu was inundated in the same violent eruptions that eventually destroyed Atlantis.[33] Thus the likelihood of finding hominid remains from Mu is nil. Finally, excavations by paleontologists in America's Southwest are now seldom performed and have typically stopped at the Clovis level—10,000 B.C. Paleontologists have found dinosaur remains in parts of America, but searches for very early hominids in America simply don't occur. The African Continent has ideal conditions for the preservation of bones, but America's Southwest has not always been desert. Moreover, scientists excavating in Africa are working under the assumption that all humanity initially developed there.

ARE WE STILL EVOLVING?

In 1939, Cayce was asked, "What will the Aquarian Age mean to mankind as regards Physical, Mental, and Spiritual development?" He responded that we would gain "the full consciousness of the ability to communicate with or to be aware of the relationships to the Creative Forces and the uses of same in the material environs." Cayce further notes that "only those who accept same [the influence of the vibratory influences] will even become aware of what's going on about them!"[34] Thus it appears that we are moving in the direction of regaining abilities we had during the era of the third root race.

The Cayce readings confirm that we are on the upward or more spiritual side of the arc of evolution, and that our choices affect that direction. We are told that we evolve through "suffering, patience, and understanding," as shown to us in the pattern of the Christ through his many incarnations from Adam to Jesus.[35] As the readings often state: " . . . the spirit is life; the mind is the builder; the physical is the result."[36]

3

Lilith and Amilius: Ancient Legends and a Plan

(Q) How is the legend of Lilith connected with the period of Amilius?
(A) In the beginning, as was outlined, there was presented that that became as the Sons of God, in that male and female were as one . . . *then*—from out of self—was brought that as was to be the helpmeet, *not* just companion of the body.   364-7

Though Lilith may seem an obscure figure in history, we have physical artifacts showing her image, written records, and even a Bible passage. The oldest work in which she appears, under the name "Lillake," is the *Prologue to the Sumerian Tablet of Ur* about the exploits of Gilgamesh, ca. 2000 B.C. The Prologue recounts a creation legend:

> After heaven and earth had been separated and mankind and the underworld created, the sea ebbed and flowed in honor of its lord, but the south wind blew hard and uprooted a willow tree from its banks on the Euphrates. A goddess saw the poor tree and put it in Princess Inanna's garden in Uruk. Inanna tended the tree with great care, hoping

some day to make a bed and throne from it. But alas, when the tree matured she found that a serpent who could not be charmed had made its nest in the roots, and a Zu-bird had made its nest in the branches, and the dark maid Lilith had built her home in the trunk.[1]

In this tale, we again find many of the symbols that appear around the ancient world: tree, serpent, and bird. In Yucatan, the Tree of Life is in the midst of the world, its roots descend into the Underworld and its branches upward to the Heavens. In this Sumerian tale, we find the serpent nested in the roots and the bird in the branches, emblems of the greater story of the lower mind descending into the Underworld and the higher mind staying in the better perspective, the wiser knowing. Lilith, in this story, abides in between these two states of consciousness.

LILITH IN JEWISH MYSTICISM

The second source for Lilith's legend is found in Jewish mysticism, notably *The Alphabet of Ben Sira*,[2] written sometime between A.D. 700 and A.D. 900, but recounting a tale that dates back to the time of the Babylonian king Nebuchadnezzar. In this account, Lilith is Adam's first wife, before the more docile Eve. Lilith considered herself an equal of Adam's, made in the image of God. She would not subordinate herself to Adam's wishes, especially lying under him during sex. She insisted that if anyone was going under someone, it was he, not she. But Adam wanted her to be subservient to him. It all ended by Lilith's invoking the name of the "Ineffable One" (that is, a name that is so sacred, it is inexpressible), which was thought to be impossible since it was inexpressible; but she speaks it and thereby flies away. Adam, disheartened by her leaving, calls upon the Creator, "Sovereign of the Universe," to bring her back or give him another; for he had already looked among all the creatures of the earth and found none to be his companion. A female godling was the only one who could be a true companion.

The Creator then instructs three of his angels to go after her and insist that she return. If she is determined to remain apart, then she must allow death to exist among her children. It may seem like a harsh demand, but her children were immortals—immortals that had lost touch with God and the purpose for existence. In order to insure they did not live forever as terrestrial beings on this little blue planet, the Creator wanted them to experience death—an intermission from physical manifestation—in hopes that during this period they might recall their original state and seek to regain it. Lilith agrees. One hundred of her children will die every day. Returning to Adam was not an option for her.

"Leave me!" she said to the angels. "I was created only to cause sickness to infants. If the infant is male, I have dominion over him for eight days after his birth—if female, for twenty days."

The angels, still concerned for Lilith, told her that if she did not return with them, then she would die. Lilith, not one to be tricked, simply asked them how she could die since "God has ordered me to take charge of all newborn children: males up to eight days, females up to twenty days?"

When their trick didn't work, the angels reverted to pleading with her. But she would not go. Yet because of their concern, she swore to them by the name of the living and eternal God: "Whenever I see you or your names or your forms in an amulet, I will have no power over that infant." The names of these three angels became powerful shields on amulets worn around the necks of infants. Their names are: Snvi, Snsvi, and Smnglof; sometimes written as Senoy, Sansenoy, and Semangelof (the addition of vowels helps us pronounce them, but ancient Hebrew used few or no vowels). Ben Sira recounts this legend to King Nebuchadnezzar when the king asks Ben Sira to heal his young son. Ben Sira writes the angels' names on an amulet and puts it around the boy's neck, and the boy recovers his health.

Some Hebrew legends hold that, because Lilith left Adam before the Fall in the Garden without having eaten of the apple, she is immortal and has no part in the curse upon Adam and Eve. Nevertheless, most Hebrew tales portray her as a demon who seduces men in their dreams. It is said that she lives by the Red Sea where lascivious demons abide. (The Hebrews had a tradition that water attracts demons.) If Lilith approached a child and fondled him, he would laugh in his sleep; and striking the sleeping child's lips with one finger would cause her to

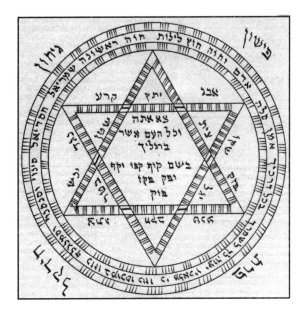

Example of Hebrew Amulet used to ward off power of Lilith—from *The Jewish Encyclopedia* (1905).

vanish. After circumcision, a male baby was permanently protected against Lilith. (This leads one to ask how then did men get seduced by her in their dreams?)

The Hebrews may have derived "Lilith" from the word "layil," which means "night." Some Hebrew traditions hold that she was incarnate as Queen of Sheba and seduced King Solomon. This comes mainly from an account which says that the Queen of Sheba had unshaven, hairy legs—a sure sign of Lilith, because in both Hebrew and Arabian folklore, Lilith is a hairy night-monster. In Babylonian and Assyrian legend, she is Lilitu, a wind-spirit, one of a triad.

The Bible passage is found in Isaiah 34:14-15 which describes the desolate ruins of the Edomite Desert where satyrs, reems (large wild oxen), pelicans, owls, jackals, ostriches, arrow-snakes, and vultures (kites) keep Lilith company. In the New Revised Standard Version of the Bible, it reads:

Wildcats shall meet with hyenas,
  goat–demons shall call to each other;
there too Lilith shall repose,
  and find a place to rest.
There shall the owl nest
  and lay and hatch and brood in its shadow.

Lilith depicted on ancient Sumerian relief—adapted from Dover.

In the New American Standard Version translation of this passage, the name "Lilith" is replaced with "night monster." The reference to an owl in this passage is significant because it too refers to Lilith. In a Sumerian relief (see illustration), Lilith is shown with owl's feet, standing on the backs of a pair of lions and holding in each hand the Sumerian version of the Ankh, the Egyptian symbol for Life. In Asia, the owl is symbolic of wisdom, particularly wisdom received in the night. We find this pertinent passage in Psalms 19:2: "Day unto day uttereth speech, And night unto night showeth knowledge." In the Roman Catholic edition of the Bible, the Book of Wisdom refers to wisdom using the feminine pronoun "she." An Asian proverb holds that the reason owls are usually seen alone, as is Lilith, is because "wisdom stands alone." In the Hebrew *Targum Yerushalmi*,[3] the priestly blessing in the biblical book of Numbers 6:26 becomes: "The Lord bless thee in all thy doings, and preserve thee from the Lilim!" Lilim are Lilith's children. The Greek commentator Hieronymous identified Lilith with the Greek Lamia, a Libyan queen deserted by Zeus, whom his wife Hera robbed of her children. Lilith took revenge for this act by robbing other women of their children.

THE REINCARNATIONS OF AMILIUS AND LILITH

In Cayce's reading of the Akasha, there was not an evil, dark tale of Lilith—simply one of equality and feminine power. In fact, Cayce reads that these feminine and masculine portions of the incarnate Logos returned to earth as some very sacred people, always working together. He lists these incarnations as Amilius and Lilith, Adam and Eve, Hermes and Maat, and Jesus and Mary. Each was an incarnation of the Logos, the Word, the Messiah—feminine and masculine aspects of them. According to Cayce, the Jewish sect called *Essenes* knew this and were actually looking among the woman of the time for the coming of the feminine Messiah, the feminine Christ, through whom the masculine Christ would be immaculately conceived. The Essenes simply read Genesis and determined that when the Lord turned to Eve as she was leaving the Garden and said that out of her would come the redeemer, He meant a woman would come first, then the man. In their temple in Mt. Carmel, the Essenes took in women of spiritual attunement, and eventually they were rewarded by a young virgin who had actually been born in the temple of an immaculate conception of her mother Anne. (See later chapter on immaculate conception.)

LILITH AND AMILIUS—A PLAN FOR A GOLDEN AGE[4]

In Poseidia, one island of Atlantis according to the Cayce readings,

Lilith and Amilius attempted to establish a new order. They established principles to live by and developed a plan whereby all could be redeemed and realigned with the original purposes and consciousness. Among their plans was a five-point assault upon the dark forces influencing this world and tempting even the Children of One. The plan called for five large groups of light bearers to incarnate in five different regions of the world and establish major centers of enlightened culture and education. Each group would assume responsibility for subduing the captivating influence of one of the five sensual influences: sight, sound, taste, smell, and touch. Each of the groups would assume some of the emotional and attitudinal characteristics of individualness represented by what we call today "racial characteristics." As noted in the preceding chapter, Atlantis would be the original place of the red race, accentuating the sense of touch. The Andes Mountains, especially the area near the Peruvian lands, would be the original place of the brown race, accentuating the sense of smell. The Gobi area (not a desert in those times) would be the original place of the yellow race, accentuating the sense of hearing. The Caucasus and Carpathian Mountains would be the original place of the white race, accentuating the sense of sight. Nubia, in the Sudan and southern Egypt, would be the original place of the black race, accentuating the sense of taste. These would set up a ring around the earth of wisdom and light.

Amilius and Lilith firmly established principles that countered those of the Children of Darkness, who now had a new leader and a sexual preference for the masculine qualities, becoming known in Atlantis as the Sons of Baal or Baaliel—or as Cayce so often called them, Sons of Belial (a term that St. Paul and the poet Milton also used). But they were not the most dangerous problem. Among the Children of the One, jealousy over the varying degrees of beauty achieved began to infest their hearts. Those close to Lilith and Amilius began to argue over who was the more important. And those who were not as close to them as they would like began to envy those who were. The insidious way in which these little spites grow within hearts and minds was and remains today a serious danger to harmony and cooperation. Before long, factions developed among the Children of One, factions that began to plot against one another's interests and influence. As bad as this was, there was an even worse development, one that even the Bible records in Genesis 6:1–4 (from the American Standard Bible version):

> And it came to pass, when men began to multiply on the face of the ground, and daughters were born unto them, that the Sons of God saw the daughters of men that they were fair; and they took them wives of all that they chose. And Jehovah said, My spirit shall not strive with man for ever, for that he also is flesh: yet shall his days be a hundred and twenty years. The Nephilim [giants] were in the earth in those days, and also after that, when the Sons of God came unto the daughters of men, and they bare children to them: the same were the mighty men that were of old, the men of renown.

Up to this point in time, there were three companies of beings:

1) the godlings who had pushed their way into matter for gratification and exaltation, using animal forms and later humanoid male and female forms to breed among themselves in the same manner as the animals;

2) the godlings who had come into the earth not for gratification or exaltation but to help maintain enlightenment and connection with the formless realms and who were conceiving new forms within themselves into which came souls from out of the unseen realms of heaven; and,

3) the zombie-like "things" that were created by the minds of the godlings to serve them and had become a breeding group of their own, in the manner of the animals.

Though Amilius and Lilith intended for males and females to come together to give comfort and oneness to each other and to conceive, it was more ideally done in subtle bodies and in accord with the Infinite One. They did not copulate in flesh bodies like the earthly Sons of Belial, zombies, and animals. This is a difficult concept to convey today because we are so physical that the idea of coupling without copulation requires some imagination, and the difference between a child of God and a child of man is not as clear as it was back then. Cayce simply compares this type of conception with that of the lowly amoeba, that pushes out from within itself another separate body, splitting its own gene pool.

In those times, the goal was to raise the consciousnesses, desires, and energies of the sons of man upward to the higher awarenesses, purposes, and energies of the sons of God, and eventually back into the Oneness of the formless realms of life and the cosmos. It didn't happen. The higher vibes and awarenesses of the sons of God began to descend further into physical matter and sensual experience.

In the sacred teachings—particularly in yoga teachings[5]—it was described as reversing the flow of the life force, energy, the mind, downward, often depicted as a serpent (representing the kundalini life force within each being) descending down a tree or staff. For example, in the biblical Garden of Eden, the serpent descends from the Tree of the Knowledge of Good and Evil, eventually ending up crawling upon its belly among the dust of the earth. This is often countered in mystical ceremonies in the ancient world by raising up the serpent energy and mind to higher levels of life and consciousness. This is the winged-serpent idea that we find in Central American and Egyptian art and mythology. It is even in some of our major texts today. Recall the teaching Jesus gave to Nicodemus during a secret nighttime visit. (John 3:14) Nicodemus wanted to learn the secrets, seeking out this strange master who was becoming such a problem for the Sanhedrin, of which Nicodemus was a member. He received three key teachings from Jesus: The first is that we must be born again. We have been born physically, but we need to be born spiritually also. The second teaching is that no one ascends to heaven but he or she who first descended from it, referring to the involution of mind into matter prior to our evolution up through matter. All of us, whether we remember it or not, have a soul within us that first descended from heaven. That part of us is familiar with the formless dimensions beyond the world.

But key to our study in this chapter is the third teaching: "As Moses raised the serpent in the desert, so must the son of man be raised up to eternal life." (John 3:14) Jesus is referring to the time when Moses left the kingdom of Pharaoh (so symbolic of the outer ego and worldly pursuits) to search for his true self and God in the desert. In his search, he comes upon a deep well around which seven virgins are attempting to water their flocks. Seven virgins in the desert—is there some deeper meaning here? Of course there is. These seven virgins, daughters of a high priest, are symbolic of the seven spiritual centers, the seven chakras, the seven lotuses within each being. Moses waters them and their flocks, ultimately marrying the eldest one. Afterwards, he meets God in a burning bush, and for the first time is instructed how to transform his staff into a serpent and raise the serpent up again into a staff (Exod. 2, 3, and 4). Later, when he has all the people out in the desert with him, Moses is instructed by God to place a fiery or brazen serpent upon a raised staff, and anyone who looks upon it will be healed (Num. 21:8-9).

The writer of Exodus is trying to convey more than a literal, physical story to us. We have to go back to the Garden of Eden to fully understand this, because Adam and Eve were not the only ones to fall in the Garden—the serpent fell also. The life force and consciousness within the descending godlings was falling to lower and lower levels. The life force can be harmful if misused, but raising it is a key to restoring the levels of energy and consciousness before the world was.

RAISING THE ENERGY OF THE BODY

In Patanjali's *Yoga Sutras* (ca. 300 B.C.), the process of raising the energy begins with an understanding of where the energy is in the body, how it is raised, and the path it follows through the body.[6] According to the *Yoga Sutras*, the energy is "coiled up" like a serpent (*kundalini*) in the lower part of the torso of the body, near the base of the spine. It moves up the spinal column (*sushumna*) through the spiritual centers, *chakras* (wheels) or *padmes* (lotuses), to the base of the brain and over through the brain to the brow. The path of the kundalini through the body is represented by a cobra in the striking position or by pharaoh's crook or a shepherd's crook. (A crook is a staff with a hook on the upper end. The shepherd's crook is flared at the very tip.)

Many books today teach that the kundalini culminates at the crown of the head, but the more ancient images and teachings as well as Cayce's always depict it culminating at the forehead, in the same place where pharaoh's brow cobra is positioned. This will cause some confusion among many who have studied and practiced for years using the crown chakra as the highest spiritual center in the body. Cayce insisted that the true path of the kundalini comes over through the crown chakra and into the third-eye chakra on the brow.

According to the Cayce material, the seven spiritual centers are connected with the seven endocrine glands within the body: (1) testes or ovaries, (2) cells of Leydig (named after the doctor who discovered them), (3) adrenals, (4) thymus, (5) thyroid, (6) pineal, and (7) pituitary. They are also connected with major nerve ganglia or plexuses along the spine: pelvic or lumbar, hypogastric or abdominal, epigastric or solar, cardiopulmonary or heart and lung area, pharyngeal or throat, and the brain itself.

A PLAN UNFULFILLED

Though Amilius and Lilith's mission was successful in many ways, the declining awareness of those in the earth was evident. Salvation was not at hand, despite all efforts. Amilius and Lilith withdrew to the deeper realms in the mind and spirit of God to prepare themselves for the next great effort. It was clear that the potential companions to the Creator were coming fully into selfishness and materiality. The plan to reverse this movement before it got out of hand had failed. Now spirit and mind were going to come fully into this world, experiencing every part of it until it no longer held any lure, and they could take it or leave it at will. The ancient lands of Mu, Oz, Og, Ohum, Zu, Atlantis, and many others were coming to an end, forcing huge migrations to the lands of the new way. After the cleansing by the legendary Great Flood, the lands of Yucatan, China, India, Persia, Egypt, Scandinavia, and others were beginning.

4

Eve and Adam: A New Body Type

For, in the beginning all was made that was made, and
as it unfolds from what man terms time to time, period
to period, there is only the renewing of the First Cause.

2946-2

According to Cayce's reading of the
Akasha, the story of Adam and Eve that begins
in the second chapter of Genesis is the creation
of the fourth body-type—the fourth root race—
for the godlings to use in their journey through
this dimension. Let's look at some of the fascinating aspects of this story.

Genesis begins, "In the beginning God created the heavens and the earth." The word
"God" is a translation of the original Hebrew
word "Elohiym," which is a plural noun for the
deity. The use of the plural form reflects the
collective, holistic nature of the original aspect
of God that began the creation. When Elohiym
speak, "they" refer to themselves in the plural,
as in Genesis 1:26: "Let *us* make him in *our* image, according to *our* likeness." Elohiym is
clearly not a singular, supreme entity separate
from the creation. God is the Collective, composed of the created ones while at the same
time their source. We actually contribute to the
composition of God. That is not to say that we

compose all of God's being, but simply to say that a portion of God's being is us. In one reading, Cayce encourages a person to come to know "that not only God is God . . . but self is a portion of that Oneness."[1]

Changing the name of God is a way of conveying changes in our relationship with the Creator. Each movement further away from direct, conscious connection changes the name. Therefore, the original creation is done by *Elohiym* in Chapter 1 of Genesis. The second creation, which occurs in Chapter 2, is done by the "Lord God," *Yahweh Elohiym*. But by Chapter 4, when Adam and Eve begin to conceive physically, the "Lord," *Yahweh*, is the extent of our relationship. From being an integral portion of the Oneness to subordinate subject of the Lord, the godlings slipped into darkness and separation.

Originally, Elohiym (sometimes spelled *Elohim*, usually pronounced *El-o-heem*) creates us in Its own image; "Let *Us* make man [*adam*] in *Our* image, after *Our* likeness . . . So Elohiym created man [*adam*] in His own image, in the image of God He created him; male and female He created them," (Gen. 1:26–27). In this passage, the Hebrew word for man is *adam*, interpreted as meaning "reddish" or "ruddy," but it also means "persons" or "people" collectively, and can mean an "indefinite someone."[2] Here adam is male and female—androgynous, hermaphroditic. It is not until the second chapter of Genesis when the "Lord God" creates adam "out of the dust of the earth"—in other words, *in the flesh*—that these sexual parts are separated. When this occurs, the name "adam" takes on the meaning we most commonly associate with this word "man"—a male whose name begins with a capital "A." But "adam" was first made in the image of Elohiym, which is not flesh. Then, symbolized by the changing of the name of the Creator from "God" to "Lord God" and finally to simply "Lord," we see the descent from direct God–consciousness to self-consciousness.

Another important point about this creation is that it is, according to Cayce's reading of the Akasha, a *group* creation—not just the creation of one famous person. At this stage of the creation, "adam" is referring to an original *group* of souls created in Elohiym's image, subsequently re-made in spiritualized flesh by Yahweh Elohiym, then into mortal flesh by Yahweh. According to Cayce's readings, the souls—those godlings within the One God—entered the earth in five places, as five nations,

and in five races; and one of these was "adam."⁵ The Bible is the story of
those souls.

At this point in Genesis, God has created everything in *thought*, in
God's mind, not physically—all existed in God's consciousness. This is
symbolized in the passage that comes *after* the seven days of creation:
"Now no shrub of the field was yet in the earth [physically], and no
plant of the field had yet sprouted, for the Lord God [note the name
change] had not sent rain upon the earth; and there was no man [in
flesh] to cultivate the ground." (Gen. 2:4-15) The heaven, earth, and adam
that had already been created in Chapter 1 were only in the mind of
God, not yet in form or matter. This was our natural home before entering the flesh. It is what is spoken of in Jesus' prayer to God, "And now,
glorify Thou me together with Thyself, Father, with the glory which I
had with Thee *before the world was*." (John 17:5) And it is that realm spoken
of when Jesus says to us, "I go to prepare a place for you . . . that where
I am, there you may be also. And you know the way where I am going."
(John 14:2-4)

Now, like many of us who are so much into physical consciousness,
the disciple Thomas challenges this statement, "Lord, we do not know
where you are going. How do we know the way?" But we *do* know the
way. Deep within us is our true nature. Deep within us we remember
the original home, and we know the way. Each of us was there in the
beginning. Each of us was originally created in the image and likeness
of Elohiym. Within us that original nature lives and intuitively knows
its way home. As Jesus said to Nicodemus, "No one ascends to heaven
but he or she who has already descended from it, even the Son of Man."
(John 3:18)

THE DARK AND THE LIGHT: TWO QUALITIES OF THE ONE

As we touched on in an earlier chapter, ancient teachings hold that
the One is composed of two qualities: that of the *dark*—meaning unseen,
deep—and from out of which comes the other aspect, *light*—meaning
seen, present, and active. In the Eastern philosophies, the terms "yin"
and "yang" are used to express these characteristics. *Yin* is a feminine,
unseen, inner principle; *yang* a masculine, seen, projected principle.

God forms Eve from Adam's Rib—from the Nuremberg Bible (1483).

An objective observation of the physical bodies of the female and male reflects these qualities. A female's sexual organs are deep *within* her torso, a male's outside his. A female body has more *inner* processes than a male, such as menstrual cycles, conception, gestation, and milk production. The female reflects the characteristics of the inner aspect of God. Thus she is a reflection of the dark, unknown, unseen, unmanifested God, the yin. She represents the unconscious, sleep, and "Night" in Genesis, thus, "the Moon and the Stars." This would also imply that the feminine is the wind, the spirit, especially since she is the conceiver, the "life-giver"—*chavvah*, the Hebrew word first used to describe the Eve portion of the original adamic being. Eve is created by God casting a deep sleep over humanity (i.e., adam), and while in that deep state, the feminine is removed and separated into an individual form.

The male reflects the characteristics of the outer, manifested God. Thus, he is a reflection of the active, changing, personal, present God. He represents the conscious, wakefulness; "Day" in Genesis, thus the Sun. He is the "tiller of the soil," the doer, the conqueror. This would also imply that he is then the reflection of the breath, the soul, especially since he is the changing, developing "doer." Our original nature was composed of both these forces in one being, but soon these were to be separated.

Adam and Eve and the Serpent—from the Nuremberg Bible (1483).

THE FALL FROM GRACE

Our fall from the original place of being is allegorically presented as the separation of the sexes and the eating of the "Fruit of the Tree of the Knowledge of Good and Evil" (Gen. 2:17), which symbolizes consuming knowledge without understanding. The Cayce readings state it this way, " . . . seek not for knowledge alone. For, look—*look*—what it brought Eve. Look rather for that wisdom which was eventually founded in she [Mary] that was addressed as the handmaid of the Lord . . . "[4]

In the Genesis story, Yahweh Elohiym commanded Adam not to eat from the Tree of the Knowledge of Good and Evil, saying "for in the day you eat from it, you shall surely die." (Gen. 2:17) Up to this point, we were immortal beings, in the image of the immortal Elohiym. However, the further we moved from consciousness of our connectedness with the Eternal One, the more we lost connectedness to the source of life. Adam and Eve began to live too completely in the flesh, losing touch with the life-giving energy. They began to reverse the flow of the Life Force, the *élan vital*, bringing it further into self-consciousness. This became so acute that, according to the Cayce readings, we actually experienced a death of the spirit.[5] To put it another way, we died to the spiritual, life-giving influence.

Another significant piece to this puzzling death was the growth of something *other than God*. The serpent in the Garden represents the mind and the life force moving downward into only self, disconnected from the Collective. It is self without regard for the Whole or for other beings. It is the self that seeks self-gratification, self-glorification, self-aggrandizement, self-centeredness. But in order for the potential companions of God to be true companions, they had to have a strong sense of self. As the Cayce readings express it: we must come to know ourselves to be ourselves, yet one with the whole (the rest of creation and the Creator).[6] In order to achieve this goal, we had to develop a sense of self—who we are, individually—then choose to cooperate in oneness with the Whole. Therefore, despite the dangers inherent in the development of self-consciousness, it was allowed because it was, and remains, the way to full realization of our role as divine companions. Yet, it often becomes a stumbling block.

CAIN AND ABEL: THE MOVE INTO TERRESTRIAL LIFE

Adam, Eve, and the serpent (all aspects of ourselves) fall from grace and lose the comfort of the Garden. The Tree of Life, symbolizing im-

Cain slays Abel—from the Nuremberg Bible (1483).

mortality, is now protected from us, to keep us from becoming eternal *terrestrial* beings when we are meant to be eternal *celestial* beings. Now we enter the cycle of life and death. This is further symbolized in Eve's conception of Cain and Abel. Cain literally means the "acquired" one (our forming egos). Abel means "a breath" or soul (our spiritually aware selves). Of course, God favors the offerings of our souls more than our egos, as symbolized in Abel's offerings as opposed to Cain's. However, Cain (ego) is angered by this and kills Abel (soul). But the Lord, *Yahweh*, comes to Cain, and says, "Why are you angry, and why has your countenance fallen? If you do well, will you not be accepted? And if you do not do well, then sin is crouching at the door [of your consciousness]; its desire is for you, but you must master it." (Gen. 4:6–7)

Noah: A Fourth Beginning

This is the point in history that the Bible says God regretted making man and began to conceive of a way to make a new start. The legendary great flood that is recorded in all the world's ancient tales was about to begin. Here is a biblical reference:

> And Jehovah [notice the name change once again] saw that the wickedness of man was great in the earth, and that every imagination of the thoughts of his heart was only evil continually. And it repented Jehovah that he had made man on the earth, and it grieved him at his heart. And Jehovah said, "I will destroy man whom I have created from the face of the ground; both man, and beast, and creeping things, and birds of the heavens; for it repents me that I have made them." (Gen. 6:5-7)

There is a fascinating past-life reading for a woman who Cayce said was on Noah's ark. In the reading, Cayce gives some insights into the coming changes in the new age that we are expecting, the Aquarian Age, and their relationship to the changes that occurred during Noah's time. You'll recall even Jesus refers to Noah's time when his disciples asked him about the so-called "end times." (Matt. 24-25) The reading begins with Cayce's mind looking over this woman's "Book of Life," her records on the skein of time and space, the Akasha:

> What an unusual record—and one of those who might be termed as physically the mothers of the world! For the entity was one of those in the ark . . .
>
> For the entity has appeared when there were new revelations to be given. And again it appears when there are new revelations to be made.
>
> May the entity so conduct its mind, its body and its purposes, then, as to be a channel through which such messages may come that are needed for the awakenings in the minds of men as to the necessity for returning to the search for their relationship with the Creative Forces or God.
>
> For as has been given from the beginning, the deluge [Noah's flood] was not a myth (as many would have you believe) but a period when man had so belittled himself with the cares of the

world, with the deceitfulness of his own knowledge and power, as to require that there be a return to his dependence wholly—physically and mentally—upon the Creative Forces.

Will this entity see such again occur in the earth? Will it be among those who may be given those directions as to how, where, the elect may be preserved for the replenishing again of the earth?

Remember, not by water—for it is the mother of life in the earth—but rather by the elements, fire.[7]

This is a disturbing reading. It seems to be saying that there will be a new destruction, like the one that occurred during Noah's period, only this time it will be by fire, not water. And it also seems to be saying that the destruction will be of such a magnitude that we will be "given those directions as to how, where, the elect may be preserved for the replenishing again of the earth."

Many of us are tired of doom prophecies, making it impossible to go on living our daily lives with hope and expectations. But Cayce's reading clearly indicates that life does go on beyond the cleansing, as it did after Noah.

5

Noah's Flood:
Truth or Fiction?

For as has been given from the beginning, the deluge was not a myth (as many would have you believe) but a period when man had so belittled himself with the cares of the world, with the deceitfulness of his own knowledge and power, as to require that there be a return to his dependence wholly—physically and mentally—upon the Creative Forces.   3653-1

The Cayce readings assert, in no uncertain terms, that the biblical story of the Great Deluge is not fiction. In fact, several individuals were told in life readings that they had been among the occupants of the ark and that they landed in the area of Mount Ararat in modern day Turkey.[1] One reading was given for a man who had been none other than Noah himself.[2] However, as is typical with the readings, Cayce gives additional details that seem both contradictory and far afield from conventional biblical dating schemes.

For example, when asked specifically for the date of Noah's flood, he gives the incredible answer that it occurred in 22,000 B.C.![3] In other readings, we are told that there were major floods involved in the partial break-up of the continent of Atlantis in 28,000 B.C.[4] Later there is a flood that occurred about the time of the

Noah gathering animals into the Ark— from the Nuremberg Bible (1483).

third and final Atlantean destruction about 10,000 B.C.[5] Interestingly, two scientists studying the accuracy of radiocarbon dating procedures have noted that there is evidence that three natural cataclysms occurred about 41,000 years ago, 33,000 years ago, and 12,500 years ago. These dates fall amazingly close to all three of Cayce's Lemurian/Atlantean destructions about 50,000 B.C., 28,000 B.C., and 10,000 B.C.[7]

The mainstream timeline for Noah's flood, based on the accounts given in the scriptural genealogies, yields two dates: 2239 B.C. (Masoretic Hebrew) and 3119 B.C. (Greek and Samaritan).[7] The latter of these two dates is amazingly close to the 3114 B.C. date the Maya give for their Fourth Creation, in which mankind emerged from waters that covered the earth. To further complicate matters, in 1997 archaeologists studying the area around the Black Seas announced their belief that a major flood occurred there about 5500 B.C. They theorized that it may be the basis for not only the Flood of the Hebrew Scriptures, but also the deluge stories found in other ancient Middle Eastern texts.[8] A subsequent study released in early 2003 could not confirm the 5500 B.C. date, but did find evidence for some overflow of the Black Seas around 9000 B.C.[9]

Other scientists have tried to verify the story of Noah by actively searching for the ark itself.

**Satellite image of Mount Ararat in mod-
ern day Turkey—from NASA files.**

**Image of Ararat anomaly first seen in 1949—from C.I.A.
files**

SATELLITE SEARCH OF POSSIBLE NOAH'S ARK SITE

The November/December 2001 issue of the A.R.E.'s *Ancient Mysteries* newsletter reported that new, high-resolution satellite images of an area on Mt. Ararat, widely known as the "Ararat Anomaly," were expected from the QuickBird 2 satellite. The anomaly was first discovered in high-altitude photographs taken by the U.S. Air Force in 1949. At the time, the curious formation became a quietly discussed secret within the CIA, but with the declassification of the photos, great interest was aroused. The photo depicted what appeared to be two structures on a 15,500-foot-elevation plateau on Ararat and even seemed to show what could be interpreted as ribs on a boat keel. The anomaly was rectangular and was estimated at 600 feet in length.

For nearly a decade, "Ark" expeditions to Ararat have been almost nonexistent. In 2001, two American teams managed to obtain permits for expeditions, but extensive delays led to virtually no actual expedition work. Another researcher, Dick Bright, did manage to visit several areas where traces of the Ark were alleged to be found. During these visits, the ice and snow were completely melted, allowing an unobstructed view and extensive site analysis. Nothing of significance was found at any of the locations visited. The government of Turkey then suspended all permits for 2002, bringing expeditions to a standstill. Meanwhile, a handful of researchers are focusing their search efforts on other mountains in the Ararat region.

University of Richmond professor Porcher Taylor has spearheaded a satellite investigation of the Ararat anomaly. Unfortunately, efforts to obtain high-quality images of the anomaly have been hampered by a heavy cloud formation that continually hangs over the area. Nevertheless, hopes that the anomaly is the remains of the Ark have faded. In late 2002, Taylor obtained other satellite images of the anomaly—but not the high-resolution ones hoped for—that cast doubt on the anomaly being manmade. These more recent images seem to indicate that unusual rock formations caused the anomaly, but a final determination should be coming soon.[10]

The Cayce readings leave no doubt that the Ark actually existed. According to Cayce, eight people were saved in the Ark. When they left the Ark, a prayer was offered. Cayce hints at the location in a reading referring to the prayer of Japheth, one of the sons of Noah: "Let thy meditation oft be that even as ye did upon the hills in Ararat."[11]

CAYCE'S STORY OF MULTIPLE CREATIONS

So how can Cayce's story containing such widely different dates for the flood be correct and what are we to believe? Amazingly, it appears that a careful study of the readings' creation story may provide the answer.

In the Cayce story of creation, as in the Maya and Aztec versions, there were four different creations. Three consecutive adams, or root races, existed over many millions of years, culminating with modern man, who represents the fourth root race. According to the Cayce readings, the earlier creations were more spiritual than physical, as our spiritual selves gradually projected ever deeper into the material plane.[12]

By the time the third root race emerged, we had really made a mess of things. Our consciousness, and thus our connection to the Creator, was so dense and animal-like that we were virtually stuck in perpetual reincarnation. The fourth adam, appearing in five places simultaneously about 12,000 B.C. (as discussed in earlier chapters), was an attempt to create a body type that would provide a better container for our full spiritual potentiality. This body would allow us to attain a higher level of consciousness and thus work our way back to our rightful relationship to God.[13]

WERE THERE MULTIPLE FLOODS?

According to the readings, the stories of creation, of Cain and Abel, and of the Flood of Noah found in Genesis are a condensed version of the entirety of human history. This history reveals a repeating cycle of creation, sin, and separation, followed by a purification process (flood). In Cayce's story of both Lemuria and Atlantis, there were several major destructions, all of which consisted of lands being flooded and continents being submerged. Also, in Atlantis there were two competing groups, the Sons of the Law of One (Abel) and the Sons of Belial (Cain), who represented the best and worst in mankind. Their struggles, the readings said, contributed to the destruction of Atlantis. The biblical narrative, although simpler, seems to parallel Cayce's story.[14]

What Cayce is telling us is that the history of mankind is not so much a linear story as a constantly repeating cycle. For example, on the current national level, as John Van Auken has pointed out, we seem to be repeating the old Christian/Moslem conflict from the time of the Crusades.[15] These cycles have occurred and are recurring on several levels at once.

Our souls experience this process not only on the historical, national, and cultural levels, but on the individual level as well. We see it in the change of seasons as the creation of spring yields to the purification of winter. We experience it physically in the aging process. It even occurs within the psychological and emotional realm, as we seem to find ourselves faced with dilemmas that, when examined, are simply old karmic patterns continually resurfacing in different areas of our lives. They recycle to give us another opportunity to overcome and resolve them—a form of purification. The Cayce readings tell us that the Book of Revelation recounts this individual struggle through the cycle of sin (separation from God) and purification within our own lives.

THE FIFTH ROOT RACE

So, if we are indeed repeating this cycle of creation, separation, and purification, where are we right now in the process? Cayce says that the present time marks the transformation from the fourth to the fifth root race.[16] Some have theorized that this will be more subtle and gradual than previous creations in that it will consist of a change in consciousness rather than in a specific body type. Perhaps it has already occurred, since we have noted that many of Cayce's ideas, such as the holistic nature of health care, have now entered the mainstream. Ideas that were once considered to be fringe or "New Age" are now common subject matter in the media. For example, a seventy-five-year-old conservative Southern Baptist friend of ours recently delighted in recounting the mysteries of the Bermuda Triangle and her belief that there must be some type of magnetic anomaly causing all of these problems.

She is also a regular practitioner of meditation, and we have shared tips on stilling the mind.

The final chapter of this book considers at some length the possible emergence of the fifth root race.

FUTURE WORLD PURIFICATION BY FIRE?

Not only are we in the midst of a new creation, but, as mentioned in the last chapter, Cayce appears to have predicted a future purification process—this time by fire. The reading regarding the deluge quoted at the beginning of this chapter was given for a twenty–eight–year–old woman in January of 1944 who was told that she often incarnated in times of great change. The reading goes on to reveal that she might be present for another purification sometime in the future and he added, "Remember, not by water—for it is the mother of life in the earth—but rather by the elements, fire."[17]

Although it appears that there may be another cataclysm, there is also a means of escape. As the readings tell us, Noah was selected to survive because he had remained connected to the Creator. He had maintained a mental and physical dependence on the Creative Forces. He not only was able to hear God's warning, but he heeded it despite the ridicule of his neighbors. We too can improve our connection to God through regular meditation and by working to become aware of those aspects of ourselves that separate us from God. Fortunately, it appears that we still have time to prepare, since Cayce seems to hint that the purification by fire is a future event potentially involving the twenty–eight–year–old woman's next life. "As to whether or not the entity will be among those in the earth when the changes again come, will depend upon the entity's preparation of self."

6

Genetics Research: Will It Confirm Cayce's Atlantis and Mu?

> The entity then was among those peoples that were advanced from the various developments during that period and was an expert in handling of the crafts of the day that made for the manners of escape by those that went to the different lands; as to the Pyrenees, to Lama [?] or Lemu [?], into Yucatan, and to the Egyptian land . . .   815-2

Since the late 1980s, a series of genetic studies has completely revised our understanding of the ancient world. Prior to this unexpected and rapidly developing avenue of research, archaeologists relied on excavations, artifact analysis, pottery and ceramic distinctions, point analysis, and radiocarbon dating. While this research has been enlightening and always fascinating, it has also led to the formulation of speculation and beliefs that took root in archaeological theory until they unfortunately evolved into indisputable "facts."

For example, from 1934 to 1997, American archaeologists professed as a fact that the first Americans entered Alaska from Siberia ca. 9500 B.C., across a land bridge that surfaced when the oceans were lowered by the Ice Age. In fact, all the ancestors of Native Americans were said to have come from Asia in this migrational wave. This "fact" completely collapsed in 1997, when a series of digs showed clear evidence of human habitation in the Americas thousands of years prior to 9500 B.C. Also in 1997, indisputable genetic evidence emerged showing that not all of the ancient Americans came from Siberia. But as the genetic research has continued, Edgar Cayce's chronology of ancient migrations from Atlantis and Mu—incredibly—has become completely reasonable and even probable.[1]

Visions of Ancient World Migrations in the Cayce Readings

The Cayce readings tell of numerous migrations of ancient peoples to various places, but primarily focus on Atlantis and Mu (Lemuria). According to the readings, Atlantis saw its beginning over 200,000 years ago, but Mu, located mainly in the South Pacific, was far older than Atlantis.[2,3] North and South America were settled by both Atlanteans and people from Mu. Cayce even described portions of the Americas as part of ancient Mu.[4] The people of Mu inhabited parts of South America and also in what is today America's southwest region well before 50,000 B.C.[5] Cayce also told of several later migrations to the Americas—by a wide range of peoples—in three stages.

The dates he gave for these movements of people were 50,000 B.C., 28,000 B.C., and just prior to 10,000 B.C. The origins of these migrations were from "the West," the South Pacific, China, Mu, and Atlantis. According to Cayce's readings, Atlanteans entered North America several times including 28,000 B.C. and 10,000 B.C. Another small migration of Atlantean descendants from the Yucatan to northeast America occurred between 3000 B.C. and perhaps 1000 B.C.

In 28,000 B.C., Atlanteans migrated to the southwest and also to parts of South America. Just before 10,000 B.C., Atlanteans fleeing the final destruction of their remaining islands went to the Egypt area, the Pyrenees Mountains, and the Gobi area. Other Atlanteans fled to the Iroquois' lands (in America's northeast), the southwest, Yucatan, and South America.[6]

At the time the Cayce readings related the above history (starting in the 1920s), all of it was considered to be preposterous by the archaeological community. At that time, the prevailing belief was that humans had been in the Americas for only a few thousand years. In 1927, the discovery of "Folsom" points pushed the arrival of the "first Americans" to about 7000 B.C., and in the mid–1930s, the "Clovis" discovery set the arrival date at 9500 B.C. The "Clovis-first" hypothesis dominated American archaeology from the 1930s until 1997 and asserted that no one was in the Americas until the Clovis people entered from Siberia in 9500 B.C.

No academic archaeologist or geneticist would dare to even attempt to publish genetic research that included speculations referring to Cayce, Atlantis, or Mu. The reasons for this are deeply rooted in the philosophy and methods of science, but also in the basic beliefs held by the scientists. Recall that American archaeology's dogmatic beliefs have been formed by excavations, ceramics and artifacts, and carbon dating. Thus, since nothing definitely attributed to Atlantis or Mu has ever been excavated, examined, or dated, both of these "lost" lands are considered to be completely fictional—at least to the American academic archaeology community. For example, the widely employed college textbook by Kenneth Feder, *Frauds, Myths, and Mysteries: Science and Pseudoscience in Archaeology* (1990; 1996), makes this blatantly unscientific and impossible-to-prove statement about Atlantis: "It simply did not exist." Feder relates that his verdict decreeing that Atlantis never existed is "unambiguous": "there was no great civilization called Atlantis."[7] But hordes of archaeologists outside the American academic community give credence to the story of Atlantis, and they routinely publish books and articles on their own theories.

Despite the American academic view, the emerging genetic evidence published in the scientific literature has fallen into a pattern that seems to match exactly Cayce's history of the ancient world. What seems truly amazing about all of this is that Cayce's many details about the specific movements of ancient people from one place to another are all being confirmed.

MULTIPLE MIGRATIONS FROM MULTIPLE LOCATIONS

At the same time the "not before 9500 B.C." idea collapsed, intense genetic research was being conducted on living Native Americans as well as on the remains of ancient Americans recovered from burial and mound sites.[8] Two basic types of DNA analysis have been done. The predominant method traces the lineage of the tested individual solely on the female side. This testing is conducted on the DNA sequence of small, energy–producing organelles (called mitochondria), found in virtually every human cell. The mitochondria are believed to be a form of bacteria that developed a symbiotic relationship allowing multi–celled life to form. In humans and animals, the mitochondria take blood glucose (sugar) and transform it into the energy form used by cells (called ATP). Like all bacteria, the mitochondria multiply on their own and carry their own DNA for this purpose.

Human DNA, found in the nucleus of nearly all the body's cells, has three billion pairs of amino acids comprising its tightly wound sequence, which extends to an incredible six feet long. It shouldn't be difficult to understand from this brief explanation that human DNA is fragile and can be difficult to sequence. In contrast, mitochondrial DNA has only 16,569 pairs of amino acids with all of these worked out and published in 1981. In addition, mitochondrial DNA is arranged in a simple circular pattern making it easier to sequence. Finally, mitochondrial DNA is not particularly fragile and can, under certain conditions, remain testable for extremely long periods. In fact, recent studies have been conducted on mitochondrial DNA from animals that lived millions of years ago. In human remains, intact and preserved mitochondria are usually taken from teeth.

The first studies on human mitochondrial DNA (mtDNA) were published in the late 1980s. Researchers trying to understand the high incidence of certain illnesses and disorders in Native American tribes began by taking samples of human DNA from tribal members.[9] For a comparison, samples of mtDNA were also taken on these volunteers. The researchers expected all of the mtDNA to be exactly the same and they were astonished when they found four variations of it. What they had discovered was that mtDNA mutated into four clearly identifiable groups. For convenience, the first four mtDNA groups discovered were called Haplogroups A, B, C, and D. Geneticists in Siberia then tested the mtDNA of various groups and found the presence of Haplogroups A, C, and D. Haplogroup B was later found in China, Japan, and southeast Asia. Initially, archaeologists hailed the findings as final proof that all Native Americans had come to America from Siberia as they had long

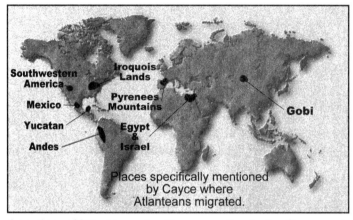

Locations of Atlantean migrations according to the Cayce readings—created by G. Little.

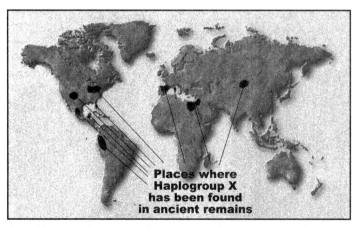

Locations of Haplogroup X recovered in ancient remains
—created by G. Little.

asserted. But research published in 1997 and subsequently confirmed by a host of studies found an unidentified form of mtDNA, which was called "Haplogroup X." Haplogroup X was not Asian. Rather, the earliest studies showed it to be possibly European. Those who cite this early research have often hailed it as evidence that Europeans settled the Americas, but more recent studies have shown a much more complicated picture.[10]

MITOCHONDRIAL DNA AS A TIME MACHINE

Mitochondrial DNA is now basically grouped into forty-two main categories called *haplogroups*. These haplogroups—or identifiable variations in mtDNA—were essentially created by normal mutations in DNA sequences. (A mutation occurs when a new amino acid pair appears in the DNA sequence.) Since mtDNA is passed from the mother to her offspring, her particular variation of mtDNA is passed on to her offspring who, in turn, pass it on to their offspring.

Because mtDNA mutates at a fairly steady and predictable rate, geneticists have been able to give fairly reliable estimates of when a particular subtype of each major haplogroup migrated away from its primary ancestors. That is, the first mutation beginning a new haplogroup can be reliably estimated by working the known mutation rate back in time. Such a process is complicated, but is well established in science. Variations found in mtDNA that are discovered in remains in one geographical area can be matched to similar variations in another area. Furthermore, because mtDNA continues to mutate steadily, there are subvariations within each main haplogroup. These can be traced back in time so that geneticists can determine when a particular variation occurred and where it first occurred.

However, mtDNA research *speculation* is based upon the underlying idea that human life evolved in Africa about 200,000 years ago, and that a series of major migrations occurred from Africa, eventually reaching the entire world. This speculation is often interpreted as fact and has led to confusion as new evidence emerges. For example, the first human (believed to have lived in Africa) is called "Mitochondrial Eve" (discussed in Chapter 2). Some writers have speculated that seven major mtDNA lineages mutated from the first Eve with the first female in each of the new lineages called a "Mini–Eve."[11]

It is important to understand that most geneticists agree with the "Out of Africa" idea, but a minority favors a simultaneous evolution of humans at several places in the world. The latter idea is expressed in the Cayce readings, and research conducted in South America in 2002 has confirmed the presence of "extinct" versions of mtDNA. In truth, the origin of humanity remains speculative, but the mtDNA research does provide a valid view into humanity's past—but only to a point.

CAYCE'S THREE MIGRATIONS SUPPORTED

In our prior books, we showed how many archaeologists and geneticists now embrace the idea of three ancient migrations to the Americas.[12,13] The dates of these migrations are approximately 47,000 B.C., 28,000 B.C., and 10,000 B.C.—nearly matching Cayce's three dates.

Genetic research on Native Americans shows the presence of three mtDNA haplogroups that originated in Asia: A, C, and D. These people, we believe, fit Cayce's description of people migrating to America from "the West." Another haplogroup found in Native Americans, called B, now appears to have originated in extreme southwestern Asia—probably in the South Pacific area. We speculated that this haplogroup could have originated from Mu. In fact, Haplogroup B appears to have been the first present in the Americas centering in the southwest and on the Pacific Coast of South America—just as Cayce stated.

Haplogroup X has now been found in both living Native Americans (4 percent) and in larger numbers in ancient remains tested after their removal from burial mounds in the traditional Iroquois land. In 2000, we speculated that Haplogroup X seemed to fit the pattern of Atlantean migrations.[14]

HAPLOGROUP X AND CAYCE'S CHRONOLOGY FOR ATLANTEAN MIGRATION

Haplogroup X has now been found in Egypt and Israel and in the Altaic Mountains of the Gobi Desert. Interestingly, Cayce indicated that the Atlanteans fled to these very areas. In addition, it is distributed in remains from Florida, the Andes of Peru, and the southwest, and current estimates are that people with Haplogroup X entered the Americas in 28,000 B.C. and also in 10,000 B.C., matching Cayce's chronology.[15]

In 2001, Spanish geneticists trying to understand the origin of the Basque people removed 121 human remains from ancient burials in the Pyrenees Mountains and subjected them to testing. Surprisingly, they found that Haplogroup X was present, but the haplogroups they expected were absent. Significantly, Haplogroup X has therefore now been found in all of the places to which groups of Atlanteans fled, according to Cayce![16]

The most astonishing genetic research seems to confirm a small but significant portion of Cayce's story. According to the readings, sometime well after 3000 B.C.—probably a few thousand years later—a group of Atlantean descendants migrated from Mexico with another group to the Northeast of America where they established the Mound Builder culture. These Atlantean descendants merged with Atlanteans already present in that area.

Astonishing as it may seem, the results of a study published in the *American Journal of Human Genetics* (vol. 70, 2002) fits all of these specific Cayce statements. The article, titled "The Structure of Diversity Within New World Mitochondrial DNA Haplogroups: Implications for the Prehistory of North America," was authored by ten eminent archaeologists and geneticists. Over 1,600 Native Americans' mtDNA was tested, representing thirty-six different North American tribes. Haplogroup X was found in the highest levels in the traditional Iroquois lands and in the Southwest—both areas where Cayce stated Atlanteans had focused their migrations. The evidence went on to show that these areas experienced sudden "population expansions" of Haplogroup X at different times. (This means that an influx of new people bearing Haplogroup X occurred.) In the Southwest, it occurred in 10,000 B.C., adding to the Haplogroup X population that had come there in 28,000 B.C. Curiously, while Haplogroup X appeared in the Northeast of America (the Iroquois lands) in 10,000 B.C., it is now believed that a new group carrying Haplogroup X entered this area about 1000 B.C. (This group could have been the descendants of the Atlanteans who went to Yucatan around 10,000 B.C.)[17]

Mu Migrations Also Supported

Since the 1980s, South American archaeologists have presented evidence showing that humans lived there as long ago as 300,000 B.C. After the collapse of the idea that the first Americans arrived in 9500 B.C., several South American sites were confirmed as being at least 50,000 years old, and many sites show reliable dates going back hundreds of thousands of years. [18]

The Cayce readings relate that while portions of South America were already occupied (a statement now confirmed), people from Mu went to southwestern America and South America in 50,000 B.C. and 28,000 B.C.[19] Since no one ever asked Cayce follow-up questions about these migrations, few other details were given. Haplogroup B, the type we speculated originated in Mu, is now known to be virtually restricted in America to the Southwest—in complete agreement with Cayce's statements. Geneticists believe that these people entered the Americas not long after 50,000 B.C.—perhaps from the South Pacific. But the origin of these "South Pacific" people has long been debated.

In a 2002 issue of *Genetics*, six British researchers attempted to identify the origins of seventeen different populations in the South Pacific. Collectively termed "Oceanic-speaking peoples," the origins of the people of Polynesia, Melanesia, and Micronesia have always been unknown. Archaeologists have speculated that a migration from Taiwan, perhaps in 6000 B.C., was their actual origin. However, archaeologists have long acknowledged that the islands were inhabited in 28,000 B.C.—a date Cayce cited. Haplogroup B is, of course, present in the South Pacific in high numbers. Testing the Y Chromosome of 390 natives, the authors were forced to conclude that these people did not originate from Taiwan. Rather, the "source population [was] in Melanesia and/or eastern Indonesia." Thus it is quite possible that the islanders of the South Pacific are, in fact, the remnants of a once large population that dispersed as its lands disappeared. These ancient people would have gone to South America and southwest America, just as Cayce stated. The genetic evidence is fully in line with this idea.[20]

CAYCE'S CHRONOLOGY IN NEW LIGHT

It is unreasonable to expect that archaeologists or geneticists will consider Cayce's ancient history as viable. However, several interesting points need to be emphasized: Cayce's readings on the ancient world began in 1923, almost eighty years before the new archaeological time-tables emerged. The dates he gave for ancient migrations—50,000 B.C., 28,000 B.C., and 10,000 B.C.—were unimaginable to academics. Now, however, Cayce's dates are almost the exact same dates that archaeologists and geneticists confirm. In addition, Cayce's specific details on the Atlantean and Mu migrations are clearly supported by the results from a multitude of genetic studies. In brief, the recent confirmation of the specific information Cayce gave so long ago would be an unlikely coincidence. It suggests that his outline of an even earlier history, and the ultimate spiritual source of humanity, may well have validity.

7

The Search for the Halls of Records: Egypt, Yucatan, and Bimini

> . . . those records of the activities of individuals were preserved—the one in the Atlantean land, that sank, which will rise and is rising again; another in the place of the records that leadeth from the Sphinx to the hall of records, in the Egyptian land; and another in the Aryan or Yucatan land, where the temple there is overshadowing same.   2012-1

The Cayce readings stated that shortly before the final destruction of Atlantis, ca. 10,000 B.C., some of the residents of that land sought to compile and preserve the world's highest knowledge and wisdom. In order to achieve this aim, three identical sets of records were created and hidden in different areas around the world for safekeeping. Cayce referred to these locations as "Halls of Records." Stone tablets, linens, gold, and other artifacts are said to be stored there. Included as well were written records that relate the entire history of humanity, including the beginnings "when the Spirit took form or began the encasements" in physical bodies in the ancient lands of Lemuria and Atlantis. They also contain information about the ancient practice of building pyramids.[1]

The readings identified three locations for the Atlantean Halls of Records: Egypt, near the Sphinx; underwater in the Bimini area; and in the Yucatan, possibly near the ancient Maya city of Piedras Negras, Guatemala. The latter location was not specifically named in the readings, but from clues and details given in several readings, Cayce researchers in the 1930s concluded that Piedras Negras was the most likely location.[2]

Over the years, the A.R.E. has actively sponsored scientific investigation at all three sites. Most of it, however, has been focused on Egypt, since the readings give very specific clues for the location of the Hall at that site. A great deal of exploration has also gone on in the Bahamas near the islands of Bimini and more recently at Andros. The search in the Yucatan has consisted mostly of monitoring the research done by various university–affiliated archaeologists at Piedras Negras and other sites.

The Sphinx and the Great Pyramid—photo by G. Little.

RESEARCH ON THE EGYPT HALL OF RECORDS

The Cayce readings describe the location of the Hall of Records in Egypt in great detail. A 1933 reading states, "*This in position lies, as the sun rises from the waters, the line of the shadow (or light) falls between the paws of the Sphinx, that was later set as the sentinel or guard, and which may not be entered from the connecting chambers from the Sphinx's paw* [right paw] *until the* time *has been fulfilled when the changes must be active in this sphere of man's experience. Between, then, the Sphinx and the river.*[3]

For over thirty years, the A.R.E. has been actively investigating an area of Egypt, near Cairo known as the Giza Plateau. Thanks to the excellent diplomatic work of Hugh Lynn Cayce, this research was allowed to proceed in spite of the skepticism of mainstream Egyptologists who have, so far, found no evidence to support the existence of a high Egyptian civilization dating back to 10,000 B.C.

Despite many tantalizing leads, the Hall of Records in Egypt remains elusive. From 1957 until 1979, the Edgar Cayce Foundation (a sister organization of the A.R.E.) worked closely with various organizations, such as the National Science Foundation and Stanford Research Institute, to try to locate hidden chambers near the Sphinx and the Great Pyramid. Although the capability of the various ground-penetrating sensing technologies steadily improved during that time period, all of the anomalies drilled prior to 1979 were determined to be natural formations in the bedrock.[4]

In 1980, the Director General of the Giza Plateau drilled into the ground in an area 165 feet from the front paws of the Sphinx and mysteriously hit bedrock at a depth of only 6 feet. Shortly thereafter, in an area approximately 100 feet away from that drilling site, a group of Egyptian irrigation specialists were checking groundwater levels and hit granite at a depth of 50 feet. They were unable to drill further. Granite is not found naturally in the Giza Plateau. It is known that all of the granite used to build the Giza monuments had to be transported from a site 600 miles to the south.

In the early 1990s, professional geophysicist Dr. Thomas Dobecki performed seismographic analysis of the Sphinx and picked up signs of what could be a large rectangular chamber near the front paws of the Sphinx.[5] In 1997, using ground-penetrating radar, A.R.E. members Joe Jahoda and Dr. Joseph Schor discovered a 25-by- 40-foot underground cavern near the Sphinx. NASA scientists verified the cavern, and Jahoda and Schor were allowed to do limited drilling in order to drop cameras down for a better look. Although the cavity appeared to be a natural formation, resembling a cave, it made what may be an unnatural 90-

degree turn. Tentative approval was given for a more sophisticated radar analysis. Then at Giza, complications arose which have, to this writing, essentially stopped this search.

The Sphinx—photo by L. Little.

WERE THE GIZA MONUMENTS BUILT IN 10,000 B.C.?

Some of the most exciting research related to the Cayce readings was
done in 1993 by Boston University geologist, Dr. Robert Shoch. Mainstream archaeologists have decreed (with little hard evidence) that the
Sphinx was built at the time of the pharaohs ca. 2500 B.C. Dr. Shoch has
challenged that theory simply by observing that the erosion found on
the Sphinx was most likely caused by water. If Schoch is correct—and he
has been supported by many of his colleagues in the Geological Society
of America—the Sphinx would have had to be constructed near the

10,000 B.C. date at a time when the climate of the Giza Plateau was more tropical.

Around the same time, Graham Hancock and Robert Bauval, archaeological journalists and researchers, published astronomical research that also supported Cayce's 10,000 B.C. date. They noted that a very important aspect of the ancient Egyptian religion was the 26,000-year astronomical cycle known as the precession of the equinoxes. The star grouping that can be viewed in the eastern sky shortly before dawn determines which of the 2,100-year-long "ages" is currently in effect. Since the Sphinx faces east and is built in the shape of a lion, Hancock and Bauval believe that it would have most likely been built when the constellation Leo was rising. They were shocked to discover that the last time the world was in the age of Leo was 10,500 B.C.[6]

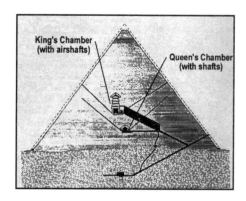

The Corridors and Shafts within the Great Pyramid— adapted from J. Van Auken's *Ancient Egyptian Mysticism* (1994).

Close up view of King and Queen's chambers in Great Pyramid— adapted from J. Van Auken's *Ancient Egyptian Mysticism* (1994).

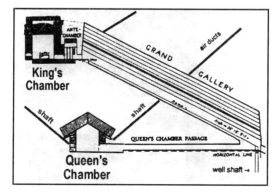

SECRET PASSAGES IN THE GREAT PYRAMID?

During the summer of 2001, two French archaeologists claimed to have located entrances to hidden chambers in the Great Pyramid. Their discoveries were reported in an *ABC Online News Service* story. The French researchers used computerized architectural data from Egyptian funeral designs as well as a technique called macrophotography to analyze hundreds of meters of walls within the pyramid. Although the two men have called for a joint French–Egyptian effort to uncover the chambers, the response from other Egyptologists, both French and Egyptian, has been less enthusiastic.

In 1993, Rudolph Gatenbrink found what appeared to be a small door, or plug, at the far end of one of the air shafts leading from the Queen's chamber in the Great Pyramid. A follow-up study was completed in September 2002. Behind that door was another similar door about eight inches further up the shaft. The second airshaft in the Queen's chamber was explored and also found to contain a door with two totally intact brass handles. Egyptian officials state that they plan to investigate further.

**Airshaft opening in the Queen's Chamber of the
Great Pyramid—photo by L. Little.**

YUCATAN HALL OF RECORDS AT PIEDRAS NEGRAS

In a 1933 reading, Cayce indicated that the Yucatan records were in a place that had been explored by the University of Pennsylvania (Penn) just a few months earlier. The readings also indicated that some Atlantean artifacts may have been removed from the site and sent to museums in Pennsylvania, Washington, and Chicago.[8] The only site being explored by Penn near the Yucatan in 1933 was Piedras Negras.

Located deep within the Guatemala jungle, Piedras Negras can only be accessed by two days of travel via rugged mountain "roads," then by canoe over whitewater rapids. Because the site is located in a rainforest, it is only feasible to work there in the dry seasons—roughly March through June. Even then, the weather is hot and humid, and the remoteness of the site allows only the most primitive camping conditions. This, along with the nearby camps of several guerilla groups, has helped to protect the site from widespread looting.

The Lost Hall of Records documents the results of our efforts to determine what Penn found in 1933. They did not uncover a Hall of Records, and none of the artifacts they found were dated older than 600 B.C. However, our research led us to believe that the Atlantean artifact the readings referred to may be magnetic stones found at the site. In addition, we believe that there are two locations at the site that could contain an underground hall of records, since these areas were especially focused on during the 1933 season.

Artist's reconstruction of the Acropolis structure at Piedras Negras by Tatiana Proskouriakoff—reprinted from *An Album of Maya Architecture*, Carnegie Institution of Washington Publication 558, 1946.

Penn abandoned Piedras Negras in 1939 so that research at the site remained at a standstill until Brigham Young University (BYU) sent an expedition in 1997. By 2001, after four seasons of exploration, BYU decided not to return, although they are continuing to perform laboratory analysis of the materials they uncovered there. During their final season (Spring 2000), BYU excavated some of the oldest pyramids located at the site. One of these appears to have a sublevel built during the Pre–Classic Maya era—around 600–400 B.C. Due to the unstable nature of the building materials, they were unable to completely penetrate to the core of the building. This portion of the site (South Group) and the Acropolis area are the most likely locations for the Hall of Records according to clues given by Cayce in the readings. Additional excavations were performed during 2000 within the Acropolis and, as in the past, were hampered by large piles of debris left at the site by the Penn expeditions.

The most outstanding find of the season was a 3000–pound carved stone panel, which had been attached to a large pyramid. Although some of the carvings are eroded, archaeologists skilled in interpreting the hieroglyphs have determined that it contains the life story of Piedras Negras' Ruler 2. A member of the Turtle Clan, this ruler was named after the founding father god of the Maya, *Itzamna*, who was said to have arrived by boat from the east. This is especially interesting since the Cayce readings state that the records were taken to the Yucatan by an Atlantean named Iltar. Although the panel was carved well after 10,000 B.C. (it is dated to around A.D. 600), it does contain a reference to the Maya sacred creation date for the "Fourth World" (3114 B.C.) linking some of the events of the life of Ruler 2 to that time frame. Given that the Ruler also carries the name of Itzamna, there may be more to the purpose of the panel than the archaeologists are able to determine at this time. The study of Maya hieroglyphics is still in its infancy and even now it is understood that their writing style was very sophisticated and carried multiple levels of meaning.[10]

Despite abandoning their on–site excavations, BYU concedes that there is still much that is not understood about the site and that more excavation needs to be done. In the summer of 2002, the chief BYU researcher at Piedras Negras, Stephen Houston, issued a nationwide alert

Itzamna (Iltar?) paddling his boat over the Atlantic—from one of the Maya Codex.

protesting a plan by the Mexican government to build a dam on the Usumacinta River that would flood—and essentially destroy—Piedras Negras. As a result, the initial dam project was scaled down, saving the ruins—for now. However, the Mexican government hopes to construct six additional dam sites on the river at some future date.[11]

THE SEARCH FOR THE SUNKEN ATLANTIS AT BIMINI, ANDROS, AND CUBA

Much exploration has been done in the area of the Bimini Islands since the 1968 discovery of the unusual underwater stone formation known as the "Bimini Road." The Cayce readings had predicted the discovery of ruins in that area during that year.[12] According to the readings, Bimini was near the place where the largest Atlantean island sank about 10,000 B.C. Since the discovery of the "road," aerial photographic surveys have turned up several other unusual underwater formations. Some of these are pentagon–shaped and others resemble building foundations. Shipwreck debris scattered all over the area has confused the issue bringing some less than scientific and greatly sensationalized claims of proof of Atlantis. Unfortunately, these claims are easily debunked and ridiculed by the scientific community.[13]

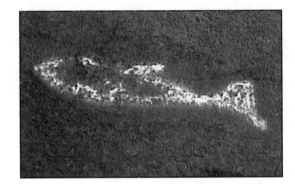

**Aerial view of Bimini
Shark Mound—photo
by G. Little.**

**Underwater view of
some of the stones in
Bimini Road—photo by
L. Little.**

Sampling of the stone found in the road formation has also turned
up conflicting evidence. Samples taken in the 1970s by the U.S. Geological Survey concluded that the road was simply a natural beach rock
formation.[14] In 1997, Dr. Joan Hanley of the *Gaea Project* reported that the
content of the rocks varied geologically to the point that they could *not*
have been located side–by–side naturally. One of the most exciting discoveries, however, was a series of effigy sand mounds shaped like a
shark, dolphin, and alligator within the Bimini mangrove swamps. The
mounds align primarily with the stars Sirius, Rigel, Vega, and Capella in
about A.D. 1000. Ground–penetrating radar has failed to locate any ar-

tifacts under the mounds, although the high water table may have created a barrier.[16]

The 1990s also brought the discovery of an additional large stone formation south of Bimini similar to the 1968 "road." In 1993, *Project Alta*, a side-scan sonar search of the area south of Bimini, reported the discovery of a thirty-five-foot-wide hexagonal feature as well as some unusual right angles, concentric circles, and triangular-shaped features. In 1998 and 1999, donations were received by the *Gaea Project* to do sonar analysis on the ocean floor near the location of the Bimini road off the Bahama ridge. In addition, a small submersible sub was employed as well as deep divers to view areas by the deep Gulf Stream near Bimini. Interesting formations appearing to be ancient waterfalls and various features were observed, but the results were inconclusive.

WAS CUBA ONCE PART OF ATLANTIS?

Since the readings described Atlantis as spanning an area from the Gulf of Mexico to the Mediterranean, the 2001 discovery of a possible underwater city near Cuba created much excitement among those searching for the Halls of Records.[17] A Canadian-based company headed by Paulina Zelitsky, a Russian engineer who was employed by the Cuban government to retrieve gold from sunken Spanish ships, located the site under 2,200 feet of water. The company had been exploring an area west of Cuba that contains a number of underwater volcanoes. It is believed that this part of the seabed once formed a land bridge joining Cuba with the Yucatan Peninsula of Mexico. It was in this area that the "lost city," containing what appeared to be pyramids, highways, tunnels, and some manmade carvings, was sighted.[18]

British researcher, Andrew Collins, author of the 2000 book, *Gateway to Atlantis*, was allowed to view both video and sonar images of the site. The discovery could provide verification of his theory that Plato's Atlantis was in Cuba near the Isle of Pines. In his book he points out that, since the 1950s, light-aircraft pilots and other explorers (including the famous treasure hunter Mel Fisher) have reported seeing submerged manmade structures southwest of the Great Bahama Bank and north of

Cuba. He believes that the destruction of ancient Cuba/Atlantis was caused by huge tidal waves created when comet fragments fell to earth about 9000 B.C.

In 2002, during a presentation at A.R.E's annual Ancient Mysteries Conference, Collins reported that he did not see anything on Zelitsky's images that he could verify to be manmade. He related that the video contained pictures of various stone "formations," some of which appeared darker in color than others, and some appeared to have smooth surfaces. Collins also stated that he did not see anything in the images he was shown that resembled the manmade carvings of an encircled cross purportedly discovered by the Canadian researchers.[19] The Canadian company is currently attempting to bring samples from the ruins to the surface, although their progress is uncertain because of funding problems.

CURRENT FINDINGS AND FUTURE RESEARCH PLANS

The A.R.E. has asked Collins to develop a plan for future investigations of the Cuban area he has identified. The Cuba connection is especially significant to the Cayce readings because of an enigmatic statement made in a 1927 reading which said that further Atlantean discoveries would be made in the future to the south and west of Bimini. " . . . for this is of the first highest civilization that will be uncovered in some of the adjacent lands to the west and south of the isles, see? Ready for questions. (Q) Is this the continent known as Alta or Poseidia [Atlantis]? (A) A temple of the Poseidians was in a portion of this land.[20]

In 2002, the Edgar Cayce Foundation sponsored a satellite-imaging project of an area of 630 square kilometers around Bimini. The project revealed two seemingly straight lines to the East of Bimini, as well as a dozen circles in the shallow waters of South Bimini. In early 2003, Greg and Lora Little visited several of the Bimini circles and the lines, discovering that all the formations were unrelated to Atlantis.

In addition, in early 2003, Greg and Lora Little made three separate trips to Andros Island in the Bahamas to investigate two well-known and mysterious underwater anomalies which have often been cited as evidence for the existence of Cayce's Atlantis. From the air, both features

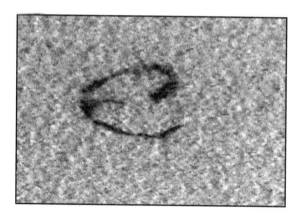

Aerial view of Rebicoff's "e"—photo by G. Little.

appear to possibly be manmade and, if so, could provide proof of the existence of an advanced pre–Ice Age civilization in the area. One of these is Rebikoff's "e," a dark formation off the northwest coast of Andros in the shape of a cursive, lower case letter "e." The second feature consists of three concentric circles photographed from the air only once, in 1968, by two A.R.E.-member pilots, Trigg Adams and Robert Brush, as they were flying over the southwest coast of Andros.

Andros lies about one hundred miles to the southeast of Bimini and is the largest of the Bahama Islands. But Andros is the least explored island in the region, and the vast majority of it is uninhabited. The Littles' investigation of the e-shaped formation and the circles showed that they were formed by nature. But two other unexpected findings emerged from the research. The first finding was of what appears to have once been a small stone structure built atop a high limestone outcrop overlooking the Atlantic Ocean. Locals call this site an ancient temple, but it is completely rejected as such by archaeologists.

The second unexpected finding was more substantial. While in Andros, a long-time dive operator informed the Littles about an underwater anomaly that, to him, resembled the Bimini Road. The structure appeared after Hurricane Andrew in 1992, and the man had seen the structure only once from a boat. Three visits were made to this structure. The initial visit located the structure and showed it to be formed of huge, rectangular stone blocks. It was flat and appeared to be between 120 and 150 feet wide. During the second visit, the Littles scuba-dived and snorkeled the site while photographing, videotaping, and measuring it. It appeared to be a three-tiered platform composed of rectangular stone blocks measuring a fairly uniform 25 by 30 feet. The blocks were about two feet thick and flat. Each tier was approximately 50 feet in width with a total width of 150 feet. The structure was aligned with magnetic north and was about 400 yards long, with one end disappearing under mounds of sand and seaweed. A press release on this discovery was issued in April 2003

The final visits to the site revealed a huge, flat area to the north of the platform. The sea bottom at this location appeared to be covered with small square and rectangular stones. The Littles have suggested that the Andros platform may have been a breakwater enclosing an ancient harbor.

8

Honeycombed Mountains and Perpetual Fires: Memorials to Ra Ta?

... until the period when there was the eventual trial of this priest *[Ra Ta]* and the companion, and they were banished into the land that lies to the south and east of this land, or the Nubian land.   294-149

There were begun some memorials in the Nubian land which still may be seen, even in this period, in the mountains of the land. Whole mountains were honeycombed, and were dug into sufficient to where the perpetual fires are *still* in activity in these various periods ...   294-150

It *[the Great Pyramid]* was formed according to that which had been worked out by Ra Ta in the mount as related to the position of the various stars, that acted in the place about which this particular solar system circles in its activity, going towards what? That same name as to which the priest was banished—the constellation of Libra, or to Libya were these people sent.   294-151

One of the most fascinating historical narratives given in the Cayce readings revolves around the life of a high priest named Ra Ta who lived in Egypt ca. 10,500 B.C. Since the readings identify him as a previous incarnation of Edgar Cayce, a great many details are provided about his life. In addition, many of the people surrounding Cayce in his twentieth–century life were told that they had been closely associated with him during that lifetime. Even though the information given concerning this very ancient era in North African history is told in bits and pieces over hundreds of readings, it is amazingly consistent and compelling. The entire story of Ra Ta can be found in many of the Cayce biographies, including W. H. Church's book, *The Lives of Edgar Cayce*, as well as in the A.R.E. Library Series of collected readings, *Egypt, Parts 1 and 2*.

Âmen-Rā.

**Drawing of Amun-Ra—from E. Budge's *The Mummy:
Funereal Rites and Customs in Ancient Egypt* (1893).**

EVIDENCE FOR THE EXISTENCE OF RA TA

The Cayce readings give several clues that could help us verify the existence of the priest Ra Ta. For example, he was one of the people the readings claim was involved in the construction of the Great Pyramid, the Sphinx, and the Egyptian Hall of Records about 10,500 B.C., a date so far back in antiquity that it has been repeatedly rejected by mainstream archaeologists.[1] However, over the last decade, some evidence has emerged in support of Cayce's construction dates, thanks to the research of Robert Shoch, John Anthony West, Graham Hancock, Robert Bauval, and others.[2]

Cayce also tells us that upon his return from exile, Ra Ta became known simply as *Ra* or *Re*, a name that is prominent in the known cosmology of ancient Egypt.[3] In fact, the creator god of the most ancient times in Egypt was called Amun–Re. But this does not in itself provide hard evidence for Cayce's story.

Fortunately, there are several geographical and archaeological clues provided in the readings that may be easier to track down. For example, in one portion of the Ra Ta story, we are told that the great priest became involved in a scandal that resulted in his banishment to a mountainous area "to the south and east" of Egypt, which the readings variously call Nubia, Libya, and Abyssinia.[4] Amazingly, the readings expound further that in 1932 there still existed concrete evidence or "memorials" of Ra Ta's presence in that land. This memorial was described as consisting of mountains that had been excavated or "honeycombed" and which contain "perpetual fires" which were still in existence.[5]

OTHER CLUES ON THE BANISHMENT OF RA TA

Two hundred and thirty followers and guards accompanied Ra Ta to his place of exile, where they remained for a period—or "cycle," as the readings term it—of nine years. While there, Ra Ta developed a closer relationship to the Creative Forces, which in turn brought peace and prosperity to the previously warlike people of that land.[6]

In fact, during his exile, Ra Ta was the impetus for several significant influences. One person was told in a life reading that he had been "a Prince of the Nubian land" and had had a positive association with Ra Ta. As a result, he developed "mysterious abilities, through chants, through charms, to bring to the people of that land an understanding that is not readily nor easily understood by those that *call themselves* of the more excellent class or group." And this ability is stated by the readings to be "a development that has stood throughout the ages—and still exists . . . "[7]

Another Nubian prince helped further Ra Ta's ideas to such an extent that he was eventually worshiped by the people of his time. The readings state that he was depicted by "statues that are seen in that land where they have the extra arms . . . " because of "his ability to minister to all phases of his own peoples during that sojourn."[8]

The readings also tell of a priestess who returned to Abyssinia after Ra Ta left and who was also eventually venerated to the point that images of her can be found "in some of the mountain fastnesses" and in "the entrance to the tombs there."[9]

Cayce further points out that Ra Ta helped the native people to learn to utilize the position of the stars, planets, sun, and moon to assist them in understanding how the Creative Forces affected "the body physical, the body mental, the body spiritual, or soul body." They even became aware of the concepts of latitude and longitude. From this, Cayce stated that the Nubians were able to use the phases of the moon and seasons of the year to master the "elements in the mineral kingdom, vegetable kingdom, animal kingdom." Thus, they began the practices of planting crops at certain times and to interact with the animals in a mystical way.[10]

Word of the achievements of the Nubians reached Egypt, and eventually Ra Ta was allowed to return to Egypt. With him was the legendary Hermes who, the readings say, "came as one of the peoples from the mount" in the Nubian land. Together, these two began planning for the building of the Great Pyramid. Cayce even states that they used the knowledge of the constellations, developed while in the Nubian land, to create the Great Pyramid as a place of initiation.[11]

WHERE ARE NUBIA, LIBYA, AND ABYSSINIA?

The first problem in verifying Cayce's story is to determine which area of North Africa is being referred to by his use of the names "Libya," "Nubia," and "Abyssinia." Modern maps of Africa no longer use the names

Early 20th century map depicting the ancient locations of Libya, Nubia, and Abyssinia—from G. Parsons' *The Stream of History* (1931).

of the last two countries. What was formerly known as Nubia is now part of southern Egypt and northern Sudan. The ancient boundaries of Abyssinia, located very much south and east of Egypt, have been roughly replaced by Ethiopia. Modern Libya lies on the western borders of Egypt, but in ancient times it was the name given to much of northern Africa including the countries of Algeria, Chad, and Tunisia. Given these parameters, the readings point to a large area in which to search.[12]

HONEYCOMBED MOUNTAINS AND PERPETUAL FIRES

In order to reduce the possible candidates in our search, it is necessary to look in those countries for areas that have mountains. Especially important would be any known to contain evidence of ancient excavation such that they might appear to be "honeycombed" and/or to contain some sort of "perpetual fire."

Also, what did the readings mean by "perpetual fires"? What sort of fire within the mountains could burn for thousands of years? It is possible that Cayce is referring to a mystical type of perpetual fire made by reducing gold or phosphorus to its purest liquid state as sought after by the alchemists. Interestingly, this process is said by the Rosicrucian tradition to have originated in ancient Egypt.[13]

Perpetual fire is also described in the Old Testament. We are told in Second Maccabees (1:18-36) of a sacred fire in Persia that was hidden for many years. Once it was returned to the Hebrew temple in which it originated, it miraculously reappeared in the form of mud that was easily ignited.

Cayce doesn't specify whether these fires were manmade or natural. He may have simply meant that the excavations were dug so deeply that they were near volcanic features—perhaps a gaseous magma vent from a nearby active volcano. Interestingly, one of the alchemist's favorite materials, phosphorus, is abundant in almost all volcanic rock.

ATLANTEANS IN ANCIENT ALGERIA?

There are some very intriguing volcanic mountain chains in southern Algeria and Chad (the Ahaggar, the Air, and the Tibesti) that contain evidence of ancient lost civilizations. Unfortunately, as a consequence of dangerous environmental and political climates, many of these mountainous areas are still shrouded in mystery, having received only scant archaeological exploration. The best example is the famous Tassili rock paintings of the otherworldly looking round-headed people, which

Prehistoric rock painting of round-headed people from Tassili Mountains in Algeria—from H. Lhote's *The Search for the Tassili Frescoes* (1959).

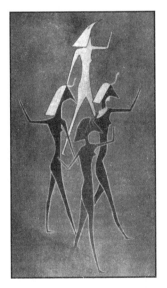

Prehistoric rock painting from Tassili Mountains in Algeria of zodiacal design similar to those of the sun temples of Ra at Abu Sir—from H. Lhote's *The Search for the Tassili Frescoes* (1959).

Prehistoric rock painting from Tassili Mountains in Algeria depicting white, brown, red, and black colored Bird-Headed Goddesses corresponding to four of the five branches of Cayce's Fourth Root Race—from H. Lhote's *The Search for the Tassili Frescoes* (1959).

are estimated to be about 7,500 years old. Among these paintings is one that researchers believe is an early version of the zodiacal designs of the sun temples of Ra. The frescoes are located in Southern Algeria near an area of volcanic formations that, because they are oddly weathered, provided use as shelters for ancient peoples.[14]

The Winter 2003 issue of the *World Explorers Club Magazine* displays a photograph of one of the Tassili paintings on its cover. In this painting, four women with Egyptian-style headdresses are depicted, and each is painted in colors corresponding to four of the five branches (red, brown, black, and white) of Cayce's Fourth Root Race. The photograph was taken by French archaeologist Henry Lhote and published in his 1959 book, *The Search for the Tassili Frescoes.* Amazingly, in his book, Lhote speculates that refugees from ancient Atlantis may have populated this area.

Tomb of Tin Hinan, legendary goddess of the mysterious Tuareg people, uncovered by Count Byron de Prorok ca. 1924 near Abalessa, Algeria—from B. de Prorok's *Digging for Lost African Gods* (1926).

The only other detailed expedition to the area was led in the early 1920s by Count Byron de Prorok, who also proposed an Atlantean link. The local natives, called the Tuareg, are seemingly of a non-Nubian racial type. Both authors describe them as being of the white race, although de Prorok comes closer to Cayce's Atlanteans in noting that they had facial characteristics similar to Native Americans.[15] However, the Tuaregs are interesting in relation to the Ra Ta story since the readings state that he was one of the early descendants of the white branch of the Fourth Root Race that had originated in the Carpathian Mountains.[16]

THE EVIDENCE IN ETHIOPIA

As intriguing as the Tassili paintings and formations are, they do not fit Cayce's description of Ra Ta's place of exile being to the south and east of Egypt. Abyssinia/Ethiopia is not only directionally correct, but it is also the only one of the three areas of Africa that contains a recently active volcano that could be the source of the readings reference to perpetual fires. Mount Fantale, located in the Ethiopian Rift Valley, is last believed to have erupted in 1820 and still has active fissures from which gases are released. It is also known for its blister formations, which have caused the earth to dome up, creating small, cave–like craters.[17] Also, a nearby range of volcanic mountains called the Nuba is believed not only to be the place to which the Saharan Nubians migrated about A.D. 147, but also an ancient place of refuge for this group.[18]

Much of Ethiopia's early history remains somewhat mythical. It is the second most frequently mentioned country of Africa in the Bible, Egypt being the first. Ethiopian kings claim to be descended from Menelik, a son produced by the relationship between King Solomon and the Queen of Sheba about 1000 B.C. In addition, it is possible that the Ark of the Covenant has been stored there since the demise of the Temple in Jerusalem.[19]

The oldest known Ethiopian city, Axum, contains the world's largest stelae, one of which is seventy–five feet high and carved from a single stone. According to Henry Louis Gates, Jr., in his book, *Wonders of the African World*, "the Persians counted it among the world's four great civilizations, the other three being Persia, Rome, and 'Sileos' which scholars believe to be China."[20] Ethiopia is also known for its unusual underground rock–hewn churches. However, despite all of these interesting

Drawing of top of giant stela at Axum in Ethiopia—from Deutsche Aksum Expedition (1913).

features, none of these settlements can so far be dated much earlier than the second century B.C.

THE ANCIENT PYRAMIDS OF NUBIA

The oldest known cultures of northeastern Africa are the Nubian sites of the northern Sudan, which includes the pyramids of Meroe. The Sudan is the area where, the readings tell us, the Christ Spirit incarnated as the black Adam during the simultaneous creation of the five races of the Fourth Root Race.[21] And one of the readings seems to hint that this fourth creation occurred sometime shortly before the Ra Ta period, possibly around 12,000 B.C.[22] This creates an interesting link with Hermes, who is indicated in the readings to be one of the incarnations of the

Christ.[23] Hermes is also described specifically as one of the "peoples from the mount" with whom Ra Ta interacted in the land of exile.[24]

Egyptologists are just beginning to explore ancient Nubia and have found much evidence to show that its early cultures attained as high a level of civilization as Egypt. For example, in May of 2002, Belgian archaeologists announced the discovery of a 30,000-year-old burial in a mountain cavern near Dandera in Southern Egypt, containing pottery and one skeleton in a seated position facing east.[25]

The second-century-B.C. Greek historian Agatharchides described an area in the Nubian Desert east of the Nile, where gold was mined, as containing many deep caverns and caves. Even more intriguing, he described the use of fire in the excavation process to break down the rock.[26] In 1998, archaeologist Dr. Fred Wendorf reported finding evidence in the Nubian desert of standing stones and megalithic structures that appear to be astronomically aligned, dating to as early as 4000 B.C. Even the conservative Egyptologist Mark Lehner concedes that these seemingly Neolithic structures have characteristics that resemble Old Kingdom Egyptian patterns.[27]

Nubia obtained much of its power and resources by serving as an intermediary between the Mediterranean nations and those south of the Sahara. Its first capitol, Kerma, flourished around 2400 B.C., although there is new evidence that a complex urban settlement occupied that site as long ago as 5000 B.C. By the time of Ramses, ca. 1550 B.C., it was included as a part of Egypt. By 700 B.C., the Nubian portion of Egypt had gained control over the entire country creating the Ethiopian twenty-fifth dynasty.[28]

HONEYCOMBED MOUNTAINS AND MEMORIALS IN NUBIA

Although the Nubian pyramids of Meroe are compelling, the nearby carved sandstone mountain of Gebel Barkal may actually more closely fit the Ra Ta story. Located on the Nile in northern Sudan, this unusual geological feature rises 90 meters, straight up out of the otherwise flat desert plain. It is 200 meters wide and is shaped like a flat-topped box with a phallic-shaped rock tower attached to one side. It is known to have been considered the home of the great creator and sun god Amun-

Gebel Barkal—from J. Breasted's *A History of Egypt* **(1905).**

Temple at foot of Gebel Barkal with pillars depicting the goddess Hathor—from J. Breasted's *A History of Egypt* **(1905).**

Re of the "first time" not only by the Egyptians, but also by their Nubian predecessors. It was believed to have been the place where Amun-Re created the first gods and where the spirit of Amun-Re actually resided—*inside* the mountain. Amun-Re has been called the Lord of the Two Thrones in that he is said to reside at both Thebes and at Gebel Barkal. Could this be a reference to Ra Ta and his history of residence in both Nubia and Egypt?

Archaeologist Timothy Kendall reports that pre-Kerman pottery has been found near the site, indicating that Nubians may have considered it sacred prior to 5000 B.C.[29] Although archaeological excavations have not revealed any caves within the mount, it is surrounded by numerous ceremonial temples, including the Temple of Amun, in which the important historical documents of the time were stored. More significantly, it is also the site of a temple to the Egyptian goddess Hathor, whose likeness is carved on its columns, thereby meeting another of the Cayce clues. Also nearby were numerous tombs and a valley temple for mummification across the Nile.

Although there is no evidence of perpetual fires reported at Gebel Barkal, there were gold mines in the area. Also, since the Egyptians called the site "Pure Mountain," there could even be a spiritual alchemical connection.

So where was Ra Ta exiled? The verdict is still out. Unfortunately, scientists have only superficially researched each of the three areas we have mentioned. At this point, it would seem that the northern Sudan area of Nubia is the most likely candidate for Ra Ta's place of banishment. However, mysterious connections can be seen in Algeria and Ethiopia, indicating that these sites may also have had a role to play in those very ancient times after the last Ice Age. It will be interesting to watch as research progresses in these areas.

9

The Pyramids: Where Was the First?

(Q) What was the date of the actual beginning and ending of the construction of the Great Pyramid?
(A). Was one hundred years in construction. Begun and completed in the period of Araaraart's time, with Hermes and Ra.
(Q) What was the date B.C. of that period?
(A) 10,490 to 10,390 before the Prince *[of Peace]* entered into Egypt.   5748-6

The word *pyramid* almost invariably invokes images of Egypt. Most scholars have long attributed the first pyramids to ancient Egypt, but some credit Sumeria with the idea of pyramids as well as building the prototype. Nevertheless, the Egyptian pyramids are typically thought of as the oldest and most spectacular. However, the past decade has seen discoveries that make mainstream beliefs about who built the "first" pyramids obsolete. Ancient pyramid structures have now been found on every continent of the world except Antarctica and Australia, and it may well be that pyramids will be uncovered someday on Antarctica.

While a common belief is that a "pyramid" is always a stone structure with smooth sides that come to a point at the apex, archaeologists categorize many other structures as pyramids. For example, both America and China have numerous pyramid–shaped mounds that are recognized archaeologically as pyramids. Many of these are multi–tiered structures similar to the step pyramids of Egypt.

Curiously, the oldest pyramids currently known in the world, dated as early as 3500 B.C., are in Peru.[1] Even more perplexing is the much more recent dating of the earliest known pyramids in Mexico and Central America. Archaeologists date the La Venta pyramid (about 100 feet tall) as the oldest in Central America, built by the mysterious Olmecs in 1000 B.C.[2] North America's first mounds (not pyramid–shaped) are now dated to 3400 B.C.,[3] and by 1500 B.C., pyramid–shaped mounds were being erected in America.[4] Why, it can be asked, are pyramids in both North and South America older than those in Central America? A complicating factor in directly answering that question was pointed out in a Cayce reading on Central America: The Maya and Aztecs both built structures atop far earlier structures. As Cayce stated, to find the earlier structures, the others—layered over them—must be removed.[5]

The Edgar Cayce readings seemingly date the beginning of the world's pyramid–building era to shortly before 10,000 B.C. Groups of Atlanteans fled Atlantis before their last remaining islands sank in a catastrophic series of events just after 10,000 B.C. The fleeing Atlanteans, according to the readings, established pyramid–building cultures in South America, Egypt, the Gobi, and both Central and North America. Archaeological finds have confirmed the presence of pyramids in all of the locations mentioned by Cayce. Interestingly, the existence of pyramids in the Gobi area was not known at the time of the readings.

Unfortunately, few follow–up questions were asked of the sleeping Cayce regarding pyramids in places other than Egypt and the Americas. While many people assume that Cayce stated that the Great Pyramid at Giza was the *first* one constructed by the fleeing Atlanteans, this does not seem necessarily to be the case. For example, Cayce stated that the first of the Egyptian pyramids were in the hills and had yet to be uncovered.[6] In addition, one other interesting and relevant fact regarding the Cayce readings on pyramids merits mention. While the readings make it clear that Atlanteans began pyramid construction throughout the world, we have not found any readings on Atlantis describing pyra–

mids there. There are a few descriptions of what Cayce called "tiered" structures,[7] but the primary descriptions of Atlantis's buildings are of round or rectangular structures.[8,9]

In sum, Cayce's date of ca. 10,000 B.C. for the initiation of pyramid building has yet to be confirmed, but discoveries keep pushing the dates back further and further. What follows is a summary of the current status of the oldest known pyramids in the world as accepted by mainstream archaeology.

According to Egyptologists, the Step Pyramid of Zoser is the oldest Egyptian Pyramid, dating to 2630 B.C.—photo by L. Little.

Egypt's Pyramid-Building Age Began ca. 3000 B.C.

Egyptologists have long held to a conventional dating system of pyramid construction that corresponds to dynastic timetables.[10] The exact beginning date of various pyramids' construction is often placed at the beginning of a Pharaoh's reign, and the completion, at the end of the reign. According to the accepted dating, the first Egyptian, pyramid–like structures were actually burial mounds erected at Abydos in 3000 B.C. In 2630 B.C., the Step Pyramid of Djoser (or Zoser) was erected, followed by another step pyramid at Saqqara in 2611 B.C. It was during the Fourth Dynasty, associated with the Old Kingdom (2575 B.C.–2134 B.C.), that the

Giza pyramids were erected as well as other well-known pyramids. The Great Pyramid of Khufu was completed ca. 2528 B.C., according to the accepted chronology.[1]

CARBON DATING THE EGYPTIAN PYRAMIDS

In the 1997 St. Martin's edition of *Mysteries of Atlantis Revisited*, the intriguing idea of carbon dating the pyramids is described: "The idea to carbon date the pyramids originated from an A.R.E. tour group in November 1982. After discussing archaeological disparities between conventional Egyptology and information given in the Cayce readings, several A.R.E. members expressed an interest in putting the 10,000 B.C. date for the Great Pyramid to the test through Carbon-14 dating, and agreed to financially support the testing through the ECF [Edgar Cayce Foundation] if it could be done."[11]

Between December 1983 and February 1984, a highly qualified team gathered seventy-one samples for carbon testing from thirteen pyramids and a tomb. The samples were typically charcoal or other organic matter found in mortar or in seams between stones. In 1986, the A.R.E. member magazine, *Venture Inward*, reported the results to the membership in the May/June issue.

Fourteen samples tested from the Great Pyramid ranged in age from 3100 B.C. to 2850 B.C., nowhere near 10,000 B.C., but several hundred years older than the 2528 B.C. date usually given. It should be mentioned that the dating of the Egyptian pyramids and the Sphinx is not truly settled and that the carbon dating does not constitute absolute proof. But it is likely that the current structures we identify as the pyramids of Giza were not erected in 10,000 B.C.

While the dating of the Great Pyramid may call into some doubt its age, it is clear that we don't know everything about it. The famous "air shafts" leading from the Queen's Chamber toward the outside of the structure remain enigmatic. The 2002 televised "opening" of the door in one of the shafts led to another door. And in late 2002, another curious fact about the Great Pyramid was released involving its composition.

Few arguments have emerged about the number of stones comprising the Great Pyramid. Most estimates have placed the number of stones between 2 and 3 million, with 2.3 million seemingly the most accepted number. The Foreword to the 1978 reprint of Piazzi Smyth's 1880 book, *Our Inheritance in the Great Pyramid*, states that "the Great Pyramid, that of Cheops, consists of well over two million limestone blocks, some weighing over 15 tons." Egyptian authorities have long quoted the 2.3 million figure as the accepted estimate, but amazingly, it appears that no one has taken the time to make a more precise count.

On December 4, 2002, Zahi Hawass, Secretary General of the Supreme Council for Antiquities in Egypt, announced the completion of a new project that produced a more accurate estimate of the number of stones. According to their findings, "The Great Pyramid of Khufu at Giza consists of one million limestone rocks." The results are hailed as a tribute to the ancient Egyptian pyramid builders, because they "were even more organized and efficient than previously thought."[12]

One aspect the recount will affect is the estimate of time the construction work is believed to have taken. Obviously, past estimates have been based on the cutting, moving, and fitting of 2.3 million stone blocks. New estimates of construction time, based on the use of only one million blocks, will no doubt be considerably shorter.

The Ziggurat of Ur, supposedly constructed in 2016 B.C., is believed by many biblical scholars to be the Tower of Babel—from *Wonders of the Past* (1923).

ZIGGURATS AND THE SO-CALLED
BEGINNING OF CIVILIZATION

Historians have long pointed to the establishment of cities in what is today southern Iraq as the beginning of civilization.[13] The Sumerians, most scholars believe, entered this area—known as Mesopotamia—from an unknown homeland some time around 4000 B.C.[14] The Bible refers to this area as the "land of Shinar,"[15] the place where the descendants of Adam—survivors of the great flood—supposedly settled. It is known that several languages were spoken here.

The Sumerians are usually—and now incorrectly—credited with being the first to build monumental, pyramid-like structures. These huge buildings were called *ziggurats* and were erected from mud bricks.[13] The first known of these was at Urek (called Erech in the Bible), located in the modern city of Warka. A walled fortress extending over a thousand acres, Urek is believed to have reached a population of 50,000. The focal point of the city was a massive, forty-foot-high, flat-topped (truncated), mud-brick pyramid structure with a temple at its summit. It is dated to about 3000 B.C. and is believed to have been the prototype of the taller step-pyramid-like ziggurats that followed. The Ziggurat of Ur, erected by 2016 B.C., is the best known, but Nebuchadnezzar II is credited with finishing the tallest ziggurat at Babylon.[1] Many scholars believe this seven-tiered, 295-foot-tall structure to be the Tower of Babel, spoken of in the Bible.[13,16]

The individual usually credited with the establishment of the first ziggurat at Urek is Gilgamesh. The *Epic of Gilgamesh*, written on clay tablets, relates that Gilgamesh was the first historical king of ancient Mesopotamia, located in modern Iraq.[14] According to the story, Gilgamesh had accumulated all the knowledge and history of the world before the Great Flood. Most archaeologists have discounted the tale as pure myth, but on April 29, 2003, German archaeologists working with *BBC News* announced that they believed they had discovered the actual tomb of Gilgamesh.[17]

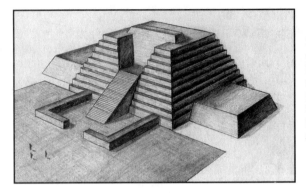

3,500 B.C. pyramid complex at Aspero, Peru, is currently the oldest known pyramid. Reconstruction by Dee Turman—from *Ancient South America* (2002).

Caral, inaccurately touted as "America's first civilization," dates to 2700 B.C. and is only one of 18 different pyramid complexes in the Supe Valley of Peru. Reconstruction by Dee Turman—from *Ancient South America* (2002).

Peru's Pyramids—The Oldest in the World?

One of the most surprising discoveries in recent years is the existence of many pyramid structures on the Pacific coast of northern Peru that date to ca. 3500–3200 B.C. Seven truncated pyramids, along with six other pyramids and several mounds, were erected from mud bricks and basalt blocks at Aspero. Many of the Aspero structures were then covered with adobe stucco, which was then painted with various designs and motifs.[1,18]

Aspero contains nearly 200,000 cubic yards of stone and mud brick in its structures.[18] The largest pyramid at the site is the Huaca de los Idolos standing 33 feet tall on a base measuring 120 feet by 90 feet. On its summit, rooms and courtyards were constructed. Another pyramid at Aspero, the Huaca de los Sacrificios, is nearly identical in size to the Huaca de los Idolos. The walls of the rooms erected on the summit of the Sacrificios' pyramid are over three feet thick.[18]

In 3200 B.C., a curious U-shaped complex of fourteen pyramids and platforms was erected at El Paraíso. The largest stood 40 feet in height with a base measuring 400 by 500 feet. The U-shape was later copied at dozens of other sites scattered throughout Peru.[19]

Between 2700 B.C. and 2600 B.C., eighteen different pyramid complexes, serving as city centers, were built in the Supe Valley of Peru.[19] At Caral, the largest mud-brick pyramid (one of seven at the site) was 60 feet high with a base 450 by 500 feet. Literally hundreds of mud-brick pyramids, many badly damaged by looters and erosion, remain undated in Peru. Thus it is likely that some will eventually be found that predate Aspero.[19]

India's Harappan Pyramids

Underwater discoveries off India's coastline[20,21,22] may soon alter our understanding of the development of pyramids, but the earliest known pyramid construction in India is currently dated to ca. 2500 B.C. Over seventy major Harappan civilization cities developed about this time, with Mohenjo-daro and Harappa as the best known. Huge, truncated, mud-brick pyramids with temples on their summits served as the focal point of these cities.[23]

China's Pyramids

Ongoing excavations in China may eventually yield dates older than others in the world, but currently the oldest pyramid in China is controversially dated to 3000 B.C. About this time, the Ch'in Dynasty began constructing royal burial tombs covered with gigantic, pyramid-shaped earthen mounds. The oldest is at Sijiazi, in Inner Mongolia in what is

Xi'an pyramid mound in China—photo from A.R.E. Press.

traditionally part of the Gobi.[24] Interestingly, the Cayce readings related that some Atlanteans migrated to the Gobi area about the same time others went to Egypt. These people served as emissaries,[25] traders, and in other capacities.[26,27,28,29,30]

The Sijiazi pyramid is formed as a three-tiered step pyramid and is covered in stone. Its base is about 90 by 45 feet. Seven tombs and an altar have been excavated in the structure.[24]

A host of other pyramid-shaped mounds exist in China, with the oldest of these dated to the Xia Dynasty (2200–1600 B.C.). The largest Chinese pyramid structure documented to date is east of Xi'an. Credited to the builder of the Great Wall of China, Chih-huang-ti, it stands 130 feet tall with a square base 1000 feet on each side.[31]

SIMULTANEOUS CULTURAL DEVELOPMENT OR MIGRATION?

The picture that is emerging from current archaeological work on pyramids is one that supports what has long been labeled as "crackpot" by mainstream American archaeology. Rather than being *the* cradle of civilization, ancient Mesopotamia was only one of many other world-wide civilizations that emerged about the same time. Between 3500 B.C.

and 2500 B.C., pyramid-building cultures emerged in Peru, China, Mesopotamia, Egypt, and India. Mainstream archaeology asserts that these widely separated civilizations each developed its own form of pyramid construction without outside influence. Yet the evidence seems to support the idea that a simultaneous migration of advanced people to different parts of the world occurred in truly prehistoric times. These people may have carried the basic idea of pyramid building with them, just as the Cayce readings stated.

10

The Pyramids: How Were the Stones Moved?

(Q) By what power or powers were these early pyramids and temples constructed?
(A) By the lifting forces of those gases that are being used gradually in the present civilization, and by the fine work or activities of those versed in that pertaining to the source from which all power comes. For, as long as there remains those pure in body, in mind, in activity, to the law of the One God, there is the continued resource for meeting the needs, for commanding the elements and their activities in the supply of that necessary in such relations.   5750-1

Cayce said this question would be answered in 1958. New evidence shows he may have been right.

Many people have speculated about how the ancients were able to move gigantic stones to erect pyramids and other monumental structures with such apparent ease. Ideas that have been proposed over the years include alien technology, telekinetic power, hundreds of thousands of slave workers dragging sleds piled with stones, sonic levitation, and complex systems of wooden levers. The Greek historian Herodotus visited the Great Pyramid two thousand years after its completion and reported that slave gangs a hundred thousand strong used wooden levers to move the building blocks up the sides after the blocks were dragged for miles up a long ramp. But modern Egyptologists have now proved most of what Herodotus wrote about the pyramid's construction was wrong.

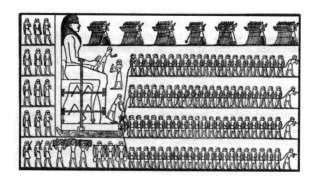

Did the ancient Egyptians drag stones on sleds? The answer is yes. This carving in a tomb at El Bersheh depicts 172 men in four double lines pulling ropes attached to a colossal statue—from J. Breasted's *A History of Egypt* (1905).

On November 12, 1933, Edgar Cayce was asked about the Mayan ruins, "By what power or powers were these early pyramids and temples constructed?"[1]

He replied, "By the lifting forces of those gases that are being used gradually in the present civilization, and by the fine work or activities of those versed in that pertaining to the source from which all power comes."

In another reading, Cayce was asked how the Great Pyramid was built. He replied, "By the use of those forces in nature as make for iron to swim. Stone floats in air in the same manner. This will be discovered in '58."[2]

The 1958 date has been used as a clue for several Cayce researchers who have also noted that another 1933 reading mentioned a "Death Ray, or the super cosmic ray . . . that will be found in the next twenty-five years . . . "[3] Edgar Evans Cayce's two books on Atlantis relate that the "maser," the forerunner of the laser, was first built at the Bell Laboratories in 1958, and a few people have suggested that this was somehow related to the mysterious force that could float stones in the air. Others have suggested that an antigravity device was invented in 1958 or that some form of electromagnetic levitation was used. Yet no real answer to the 1958 date or the mysterious "floating" force that Cayce described has been found—until now.[4,5]

The capstone from the Pyramid of Amenem may depict a "bird" motif sail, which lifted it to the apex—from J. Breasted's *A History of Egypt* (1905).

Enlargement of the "bird" motif sail.

Did the Egyptians understand the use of sails and pulley systems? In the Del El-Bahri Temple at Thebes, Queen Hatshepsut is depicted in sailboats with pulleys—from J. Breasted's *A History of Egypt* (1905).

HAS THE SOLUTION BEEN FOUND?

On June 23, 2001, a small group of researchers from Caltech (California Institute of Technology) raised a fifteen-foot, 6,900-pound obelisk into a stable, vertical position in the Mohave Desert in just twenty-five seconds. They used only what was initially described as a "kite," a pulley system, and a wooden support frame. The kite was actually a modified ascending parachute made of nylon.

The idea for the project was the brainstorm of Dr. Maureen Clemmons, who now ardently believes that the ancients used such a method to easily and quickly drag stones up ramps, float stones across the deserts, and place obelisks upright. Clemmons' team began their research in 1997 finding that small parasails could easily lift eight-foot long redwood logs upright in moments. With only a little experience, the team was able to walk dangling (floating) logs around a field. Soon they easily lifted an 800-pound obelisk to a 40-degree angle. After obtaining stronger line, the team then raised the obelisk upright from a horizontal position. The actual lifting of the obelisk took mere seconds, startling the team.

By 2001, Clemmons' group could easily move blocks of stone around with the airfoil, and a 3.5-ton obelisk was raised in front of representatives from all the major media. In late September 2001, Mexico's University del Sol joined the project and plans are in progress to demonstrate how 300-ton Egyptian obelisks could have been raised the same way. In addition, numerous groups are exploring the commercial applicability of the method.

Since the average weight of the one million stones[6] comprising the Great Pyramid is 5,000 pounds, it seems proven that many of the stones *could* have been floated to the building site by some form of airfoil. Clemmons' attention then turned to finding some form of proof that

Lift off of the Caltech kite—photo courtesy of Dr. M. Clemmons.

Ancient Egyptians may have used wind energy to quickly move building blocks up ramps at the Great Pyramid —drawing by Dee Turman.

such a system may have been employed by the ancient Egyptians and what materials they used.

Egyptian Clues

Throughout her research, Clemmons kept a meticulous journal of her team's experiences and findings.[7] One of the most curious events that took place related to the discovery of a method that could hold the parasail lines safely and also provide control. Modern ascending parachutes (or parasails) usually use a metal "carabiner" for control—but Clemmons wanted to see if the ancient Egyptians might have had the answer to line control. Looking through Egyptian paintings and carvings, Clemmons saw the solution: *Ankhs* were usually depicted in the hands of the winged birds in the paintings as well as being prominent objects in other carvings, suggesting something more than decoration or a religious symbol. She also noticed that the *ankhs* were usually shown with a rope or line dangling on them. In 1999, Clemmons tried a brass *ankh* as her line control mechanism. It worked perfectly.

Solving how the Egyptians might have made airtight sails proved easy. Linens made by Egyptians could be sealed with only a few coats of shellac. Clemmons soon found that the scarab beetle produces shellac, and she found paintings showing the effluent being collected from a beetle. The last pieces of evidence came from other archaeological finds and carvings. Sleds that could have been used to drag heavy stones have been recovered in excavations, and pulley systems were in use on ancient Egyptian ships. Finally, in a Cairo museum, Clemmons found a bas-relief carving of wings that do not resemble those of any living bird. Directly below the bird are several men standing near vertical objects that appear to be ropes.

What Was the **1958** Discovery?

The simplicity of this method has disappointed a lot of people looking for a more esoteric solution to the mystery of the pyramid's building method. But the research has also raised the ire of skeptics who, oddly, have openly derided the effort.

Despite the stunning results of this research, it is interesting how closely the "ascending parachute" lifting system Clemmons discovered fits Cayce's statement that the ancients used natural "lifting forces of those gases." Also, Cayce stated that the power came from the source from which all power comes. The sun, of course, ultimately produces the winds, and, properly utilized, the wind may provide the most powerful lifting forces in nature. The sun and winds may well be the force Cayce described as the source from which all power comes. In other readings, Cayce commented that the ancients made hot-air balloons out of skins and other materials. This assertion from the Cayce readings appears to have been confirmed by researchers in Peru.[8] So it seems reasonable to suggest that the ancients could have floated huge stones in the air utilizing a parafoil or ascending parachute. But how does Cayce's date of 1958 fit into the picture?

Cayce was fairly specific in stating how the stones of the Great Pyramid were moved. He stated: "By the use of those forces in nature as make for iron to swim. Stone floats in air in the same manner. This will be discovered in '58."

Iron swims (or floats) by the displacement of its weight in water. A ship (whether constructed of iron or anything else) is constructed so that its interior encloses sufficient space to displace more than its weight in water. *Webster's Collegiate Dictionary* even defines "swim" by the term "float." So, how can stone float in the air using the same principle? The answers and the story behind them are astonishing in their simplicity. The story relates to the development of gliders and parachutes. Both were used in World Wars I and II, but showed limited usefulness. Parachutes were almost impossible to control and only slowed descent. Parachutes could be towed behind boats or automobiles, but they provided no lift on their own. Gliders were controllable, but required a huge expenditure of energy to get them aloft. What was needed was some method that could provide lift using only the wind and a means of easy control.

In 1954, the editor of a British gliding magazine wrote an article suggesting that an "ascending parachute" could be developed to lift people off the ground. This article caused aeronautical engineers to start working on the problem. In 1958, the year Cayce predicted the discovery would be made, a "secret weapon" was developed and unveiled by the U.S. military. It consisted of several technical modifications in a parachute (the sleeve and blank gore modification), creating "lift" and giving "amazing control" under the canopy. This discovery led to the sports of parasailing and paragliding, which emerged in 1961.

Amazingly, until 1958, no one had discovered how to construct a parachute that had inherent "lifting properties"—the ability to raise large, heavier-than-air objects by displacing air—and control. It was this same technology that was used by the Caltech researchers in raising the obelisk and, theoretically, air displacement can provide sufficient lift to "float" objects of incredible weight.

It has long been assumed that Cayce's prediction about a 1958 discovery was in reference to something that would border on the incredible. Yet, Cayce's original prediction about the 1958 discovery never said that it would be widely recognized or seen as amazing. He only told us that the secret would be discovered in 1958. In truth, the developments in 1958 were incredible to those in the field of parachuting. But it has taken over forty years for that discovery to prove that stone can be floated in the air. Is this the solution to Cayce's mysterious force that can float stones?

11

The Pyramids: Who Built Teotihuacán?

With the injection of those of greater power in their activity in the land, during that period as would be called 3,000 years before the Prince of Peace came, those peoples that were of the Lost Tribes, a portion came into the land; infusing their activities upon the peoples from Mu in the southernmost portion of that called America or United States, and then moved on to the activities in Mexico, Yucatan, centralizing that now about the spots where the central of Mexico now stands, or Mexico City. Hence there arose through the age a different civilization, a *mixture* again.   5750-1

For centuries, explorers and scientists have pondered the mystery of who built the ancient city of Teotihuacán in Central Mexico, just north of present-day Mexico City. Even the Aztecs, who used it as a place of religious pilgrimage, were unable to identify the builders. They found it already abandoned when they arrived in the thirteenth century A.D. and named it Teotihuacán, "the place where men become gods." They believed that the gods had gathered there to create the sun and the moon. It was also the place where the gods began the "fifth sun" or the creation of the fifth world, each world being an era of time that ended with a worldwide catastrophe. Interestingly, the Aztecs, who were the dominant culture in Central Mexico when the Spanish first arrived, claimed to have originated from an island in the East they called Aztlán. Many have noted the similarity to Atlantis.

View of the Avenue of the Dead and the Pyramid of the Sun from top of the Pyramid of the Moon at Teotihuacán—photo by L. Little.

Modern archaeological investigations of Teotihuacán, which started in 1934, have only just begun to reveal its secrets. The site is well known among tourists in Mexico for its giant pyramids, two of which are the largest in all of the Western Hemisphere. The Pyramid of the Sun is 200 feet tall and has a base as large as that of the Great Pyramid of Giza in Egypt. Built in A.D. 100, it is the oldest major structure at this site, which was originally settled about 200 B.C.

Three other features—the slightly smaller Pyramid of the Moon, the three-mile-long Avenue of the Dead, and the Temple of Quetzalcóatl (the feathered serpent)—also highlight the eleven-acre ceremonial plaza area. Surrounding this central area are an amazing 2,200 ancient "apartment" complexes. Archaeologists estimate that as many as 200,000 people resided in the city by A.D. 500. However, it was mysteriously abandoned about A.D. 700, possibly because of the arrival of a more "barbarian" culture, the Toltecs.[1]

In 2002, a team of acoustical experts concluded that the main pyramids at Chichén Itzá, Uxmal, and Teotihuacán were specifically designed to produce an echo that matches the "chir-roop" sound of the sacred quetzal bird. A handclap made from directly in front of the base of these pyramids creates the birdcall-like echo. The researchers note that the lower steps are unusually short and have a high riser. Sound reflected from these steps makes a high-pitched "chir" sound, while the higher steps create the lower pitched "roop" sound. They were also able to pick up echoes from other locations around the pyramids that corresponded with "different musical tones spanning half an octave." They speculate that these sounds were deliberately designed within the architecture for use during religious ceremonies.[2]

Manmade Underground Passages

Engineers, archaeologists, ethnologists, and archaeoastronomers who have studied Teotihuacán marvel at its careful and deliberate design. Some believe that the ceremonial center was set up as a sacred copy of the cosmos, representing the upper (sky), middle (earth), and underworlds. Underground passageways that honeycomb the site represent the underworld. Although most sources describe these as natural caves created by volcanic activity, a joint 1996 study done by the University of Mexico and Ohio University show that these are actually manmade tunnels. Some appear to have been constructed in a deliberate grid pattern to underlie the main pyramids, temples, and plazas. First discovered in the 1940s, the caverns appear to have been used for burials and sacred rituals and for storing food and grains. Interestingly, the 1996 study concluded that the volcanic rock removed from the tunnels was used to build all but one of the major structures. For an unknown reason, the Pyramid of the Sun, the largest and oldest of the major structures, was built using only surface materials.[3]

The Sacrifice of War Captives

Teotihuacán was an exceptionally well-organized metropolis, which, at its peak, dominated all of Mesoamerica (Central Mexico, Guatemala, Yucatan, Honduras, and Belize). Its influence has been noted in Maya

sites as far away as Kaminaljuyú and Tikal in Guatemala, and just recently has been connected to Maya sites in the Northern Yucatan (at
Chac near Uxmal).[4] Maya hieroglyphic expert David Freidel states in his
book *Maya Cosmos* that in A.D. 400, "turbaned and tasseled" emissaries
from Teotihuacán visited the Maya site of Tikal. It is believed that they
introduced the idea of taking captives for human sacrifice, which resulted in a Mesoamerican "world war" and very likely led to the demise
of the Classic Maya civilization about A.D. 900. The presence of the
Teotihuacán influence is found in the symbols of the serpent and the
goggle–eyed rain god Tláloc.[5]

**Symbolic sculpture of the feathered-serpent Quetzalcóatl
(left) and the rain god Tlaloc (right) at Teotihuacán—
photo by L. Little.**

TEOTIHUACÁN BUILDERS: REMNANTS OF THE LOST TRIBES?

In a 1933 reading in which he was asked to give the origins of the Maya culture, Cayce stated that the culture was a combination of several older cultures, including Atlanteans, South Americans (who were of partly Lemurian descent), indigenous peoples, and "those peoples that were of the Lost Tribes" (of presumably Israel). The last were said to have arrived by boat from across the ocean about 3000 B.C. They initially arrived in the southern U.S., but later settled in Central America near Mexico City. Sometime even later, Cayce states they migrated into North America with some of the Atlantean descendants and became a part of the Mound Builders culture. In the same reading, Cayce mentions that Mayan altars were eventually used for human sacrifice because of what he terms "the injection of the Mosaic." Most people have assumed that this refers to a Hebrew influence from the Lost Tribes.[6]

THE BOOK OF MORMON

Another intriguing connection to Teotihuacán and the Lost Tribes is found in the *Book of Mormon*, which, according to believers, was revealed to Joseph Smith by an angelic being in the mid-1820s. It tells of both Pre-Hebrew and Hebrew Semitic peoples migrating to Central America—the former group coming after the fall of the Tower of Babel and the latter at the time of the Assyrian/Babylonian captivity, ca. 600 B.C.

Mormon archaeologist John Sorenson believes that two of these groups landed on the Pacific coast of modern Guatemala. The oldest migration may have settled in Central Mexico, possibly influencing the Zapotec culture at Monte Alban in Oaxaca and the Olmec culture near La Venta on the Gulf Coast. The latter group migrated to the Maya areas of Guatemala. A third migration, about 600 B.C., is not as well known, but is believed to have settled in Central Mexico like Cayce's Lost Tribes, after stopping first in the southern United States.

The resurrected Christ supposedly visited the 600 B.C. Hebrew group about A.D. 33 and left, promising to return some day. Sorenson and others have noted the similarity to the legend of the Christ-like Quetzalcóatl (the feathered serpent) of Teotihuacán, who was said to have been a highly spiritual teacher from the East. The fact that the serpent is feathered is believed by Mormon scholars to symbolize the resurrection. When Quetzalcóatl left, he also promised to return, causing the Aztecs to mistake the Spanish conquest for this event. In addition, Sorenson notes that the 600 B.C. group sought to throw off much of their former culture, but did maintain "the law of Moses," which may have given the serpent (via Moses' staff) a spiritual connotation. The serpent symbol eventually became associated with war and brutality at Teotihuacán (and later at sites such as Chichén Itzá) and may have been influenced by highly warlike portions of the Mormon Lost Tribes who broke from the main group. Both of these Mormon civilizations were destroyed by civil war about A.D. 400.[7]

Interestingly, the waking Cayce commented in a letter that he believed the Mormons " . . . have a great deal of truth . . . " and that the founders may have been reincarnated members of the Lost Tribes.[8] Although both Cayce's story and the Mormon narrative are very controversial in scientific circles, there is growing evidence to support them. For example, genetic testing and the discovery of Old World artifacts in the Americas have made the idea of pre–Columbian transoceanic migrations increasingly credible.

In the American edition to his 2002 book entitled *1421: The Year China Discovered America*, British author Gavin Menzies documents several archaeological discoveries supporting his theory of pre–Columbian voyages to both North and South America. He also claims that archaeologist William Niven uncovered the body of a Chinese or Mongolian person in 1911, near the base of the Pyramid of the Sun at Teotihuacán. The tomb was arranged according to traditional Chinese custom and contained both Chinese inscriptions and a necklace of a type of jade found only in China.

Although the migration of other cultures to the Americas is one possible explanation for the founding of Teotihuacán, the Cayce readings make it clear that there was a fairly advanced civilization already present in that part of the world as far back as 10,500 B.C. And even further, we are told that this civilization interacted frequently and closely with many other ancient cultures such as Egypt, China, and India.[9] If the evidence for Cayce's story of pre–Columbian (and even pre–Ice Age civilizations) continues to be supported, it would certainly shed much light on the mystery of the founding of Teotihuacán.

12

The Great Wall of Peru and the Mysterious Ohums: Cayce on South America

We also find that entering into Og, or those peoples that later became the beginning of the Inca, or Ohum [Aymara?], that builded the walls across the mountains in this period . . .   364-4

One of the most interesting and unique Cayce readings on ancient South America was given on February 16, 1932, telling of a people who built "walls across the mountains."[1] W. H. Church's book *Edgar Cayce's Story of the Soul* sets the stage for the reading's context by stating, "The first exodus of Atlanteans to other lands occurred as early as 28,000 B.C., following the second of the upheavals. Colonies were initially established in what is now Peru, but was then called Og by the colonizing Atlanteans . . . " Church adds, "Any earlier arrivals, whether they had crossed overland into Brazil or remained nearer the coastal areas, would presumably have originated in Lemuria, not Atlantis."[2]

Church's chronology of Atlantis' three destructions (ca. 50,000 B.C., ca. 28,000 B.C., and ca. 10,000 B.C.) is consistent with that of Edgar

Evans Cayce[3] and our own. Recent archaeological evidence shows that several parts of South America were occupied prior to 50,000 B.C., with probable mass migrations into the continent centering on the three time periods given by Cayce for Atlantis's breakup and final destruction.[4] This evidence is all consistent with Cayce's readings. For example, Cayce's contention that South America was occupied prior to 50,000 B.C. has been verified in Brazil and southern Mexico. In addition, a great deal of evidence supports the contention that a large migration of people came into South America after 50,000 B.C. For instance, the *Radiocarbon Database for the Andes* lists thirty-three different carbon dates obtained at Andes' excavations showing the sites were inhabited between the years 40,000 B.C. and 30,000 B.C. Nine additional radiocarbon dates show human occupation from 47,000 B.C. to 40,000 B.C. (Note that radiocarbon dating cannot be used to test materials older than 50,000 years.)[5]

Church relates that, in 28,000 B.C., "in Peru, the settlers founded the peaceful empire of the Ohums, a tribal designation probably derived from the name of the ruling Atlantean family among their numbers . . . It was the Ohums, in their dual desire for an isolated as well as secure existence, who *'builded the walls across the mountains in this period,'* we are told [reading 364-4, emphasis added]—monolithic barriers of stone and adobe, some fifteen feet wide and high, and running as far as fifty miles in length, which have mystified researchers to this day."[6]

Carlson's 1970 A.R.E. Press booklet, *The Great Migration*, relates that the Ohums were originally from Mu and were a peaceful group governed by a weak ruler. When Atlanteans migrated to the Ohum lands, they quickly became the ruling class, bringing with them the ongoing battles between Atlantis's factions—creating the impetus for building defensive walls. Thus the origin of the Ohums is murky, but within the Cayce community, there is agreement that migrating Atlanteans eventually became the rulers of the Ohums. Carlson also cites the reading on the building of the walls across the mountains, but makes no other mention of it.

The Great Wall of Peru photographed by Shippee-Johnson—from Bureau of Ethnology, U.S. Govt. Printing Office, *Handbook of South American Indians* (1949).

In our book *Ancient South America*, we related "that the Og were the ancestors of the Ohum who were in turn the forerunners of the Inca in *South America*," and we reproduced the photo accompanying this chapter.[7] It shows the walls across the mountains (described in reading 364-4), but it is not known through archaeological excavations exactly when these walls were built or the identity of the builders.

DISCOVERY OF THE WALLS

Prior to the 1930s, archaeologists believed the walls to be small and insignificant structures, because their true size and extent were not recognized from the ground. But in 1931, geologist Robert Shippee and Lt.(USN) George Johnson (the photographer) conducted the first aerial survey of Peru. The survey began over Peru's Santa River delta and went east. Not long after takeoff, Shippee and Johnson spotted and pho-

tographed the wall that immediately became known in America as the
"Great Wall of Peru." After following the wall fifty miles inland into the
Andes, a second—but closer—aerial survey was made of the structure.
This time, they noticed that a series of circular and rectangular forts
were attached to the wall. Intrigued by their find, Shippee and Johnson
arranged an arduous land expedition to the wall. They wrote that it
"now averages about 7 feet in height. It is built of broken rocks set
together with adobe cement . . . In occasional places, as seen from the
air, the wall must still be 20 or 30 feet high where it crosses gullies . . .
We estimated that, in its original state, it was about 12 or 15 feet thick at
the base and was built to taper upward to an average height of 12 or 15
feet." Some of the forts along the wall were huge. One measured 200 by
300 feet, with 15-foot-high walls remaining around it.[8]

Shippee and Johnson also found strange, miles-long linear formations of pits on the ridges of the mountains surrounding the Pisco Valley. Each pit was over three feet wide and three feet deep. Others have
found a host of Peruvian sites with these linear pits, with some, curiously, enclosed by walls.

The discovery of the walls by Shippee and Johnson was widely reported in the United States. *The New York Times*, for example, ran articles
on May 5, 1931 ("Fliers report finding Great Wall of Peru") and on August 12, 1931, when the two explorers returned to the States. In 1932,
Science News Letter, Popular Science, National Geographic Magazine, and the
Smithsonian all published reports and photos of the walls.

Some writers have suggested that the Great Wall of Peru was not
discovered until the 1950s or 1960s—well after Cayce's death in 1945.
But Cayce's 1932 reading with the statement about the walls seems to
indicate that the listeners knew exactly what he was describing. For
example, there were no follow-up questions on it. In addition, Church's
description of the walls (as adobe and stone—fifteen feet tall, fifteen feet
wide, fifty miles in length) exactly matches Shippee and Johnson's 1932
article and the description in the 1931 newspaper articles on the discovery.

MORE WALLS DISCOVERED

The idea that long walls crossing the mountains in Peru was not known until after Cayce's death appears to have been created by the later discovery of more mysterious walls. In the 1960s, Gene Savoy found a previously unreported wall in the Nepena Valley of Peru. Savoy wrote, "It originated near the coast with a group of walls that coursed inland over the rolling hills and finally narrowed to a single wall that ran across the coastal desert among spurs of the Andes, where it was lost in the uplands behind Moro." A few days later, Savoy found more walls to the south—in the Casma Valley.[9]

Perhaps the most astonishing discovery was made in the early 1980s by archaeologist Franklin Paddock, which he reported in a 1984 issue of *Archaeology*, under the title "The Great Wall of the Inca." Paddock managed to observe several portions of a stone wall extending for 150 miles from Peru to Bolivia. It was constructed at altitudes of 8,000 to 12,000 feet, but most portions were only a few feet high. Virtually no professional reports on the wall have been made since that time.

WHO BUILT THE WALLS?

In *The Great Migration*, Carlson suggests that the Aymara people, centered in the area of Cuzco and Lake Titicaca, could have been the Ohums. The Aymara people appear to have been the first population placed under Inca rule, and the walls discovered by Paddock in the 1980s are in the Aymara region. But the walls mentioned by Cayce are on the Pacific Coast of Peru. Archaeologists attribute the oldest of these walls to the Chimú culture. Beginning in about 500 B.C., the early Chimú are believed to have built walls as protection until later phases of the culture erected massive, fortified palace compounds surrounded by outer walls. The pinnacle of this effort was achieved at Chan–Chan in A.D. 900. Chan–Chan was built with nine to twelve rectangular citadels or palaces, each surrounded by thirty-foot adobe walls. The nearly eight-square-mile city of Chan–Chan was itself walled and fortified to enclose the palaces. With Chan–Chan as their capital, the Chimú established numerous outposts in Peru in the later stages of their culture.

One of the primary characteristics of these outposts was the construction of huge, mud-brick pyramids. Pacatnamú, for example, had thirty-seven pyramids within its compound. In 1475, Chan-Chan and Chimú collapsed, with their sudden defeat by the Inca.

In truth, there has been little serious effort by archaeologists to date the mysterious walls. It has simply been assumed that the Chimú built most of them, but there is evidence that the walls were built in successive stages and were probably used by a series of cultures. Exactly when the initial construction stage began is unknown, because none of the walls has been excavated and subjected to dating methods. In fact, South American archaeologists date the emergence of the first identifiable culture in Peru (the Ayacucho) to 23,000 B.C. From that remote time until 1470, at least twenty-three different civilizations have been identified in Peru.

Aerial photo from the 1930s showing the citadel-palace compounds of Chan-Chan—from Bureau of Ethnology, U.S. Govt. Printing Office, *Handbook of South American Indians* (1949).

Cayce Revisited

From his interpretation of the Cayce readings, W. H. Church relates that people from Mu apparently came to the Pacific Coast of South America prior to 28,000 B.C. This suggestion, we believe, has nearly irrefutable support from recent genetic evidence coming from investigations of ancient remains recovered in that area.[10] (See earlier chapter on genetic research.) New archaeological finds confirm the presence of humans in Peru and other parts of South America well before 28,000 B.C. and show a primitive culture of cave dwellers who left little behind other than stone implements and cave drawings. The emergence of "identifiable cultures" in Peru—by 23,000 B.C.—seems to indicate that advanced groups migrated into the Pacific Coast area around that time. What is interesting is that several other cultural groups were in other parts of South America before 23,000 B.C. Could these people have been wandering groups of Atlanteans who mixed with the less advanced people already living on the continent?

One of the most complete myths of all South American cultures involves the origin of the Chimú. According to the myth, their founder, Tacaynamu, came from the north on a raft with his family. After landing in Peru, he sent his sons in different directions to subjugate the less advanced, more peaceful cultures already present in the area. They eventually established Chan–Chan as their capital and built a great empire that lasted until their defeat by the Inca.

According to Cayce, the Ohums were ruled by a group of colonizing Atlanteans who built the walls for safety. Since archaeologists believe that the Chimú constructed the walls and also believe that their origin myth of coming from the north is accurate, Cayce's mysterious Ohums could well have been the Chimú people. And their defeat by the Inca (also a remnant of people fleeing the destruction of Atlantis) would seem to be a continuation of some of the ongoing battles Cayce described as happening in Atlantis before it vanished.

We may never know exactly who the mysterious Ohum people were. But genetic research is rapidly giving us an intriguing picture of the remote past that seems to get closer and closer to the once impossible history that was told in the Cayce readings. For example, the evidence strongly supports the idea that a peaceful group of people migrated to South America from the South Pacific beginning just after 50,000 B.C. continuing well beyond 28,000 B.C.—just as Cayce related. These people joined with a mixture of other peoples who came from the north, seemingly from Siberia, and others who came from "unknown" places. But one of the most intriguing things about Cayce's readings on ancient North and South America is that, when Cayce gave these readings (the 1930s), the dates seemed simply preposterous. At that time, archaeologists asserted that no one was in the Americas before 4000 B.C. and no one had migrated to America from the South Pacific.

13

Cayce's Ancient India: Has It Been Discovered?

Before that we find the entity was in the land now known as the Indian and Egyptian, during those periods when there were the gatherings of those from many of the lands for the correlating of the truths that were presented by Saneid in the Indian land, by Ra Ta in the Egyptian land, by Ajax from the Atlantean land, by those from the Carpathian land, by those from the Pyrenees, by those from the Incal and those from the Oz lands, and by those from that activity which will again be uncovered in the Gobi land.   987-2

Before that we find the entity was in the Egyptian and the Indian land. For with the teachings that were set during those periods of the compilations of the tenets and truths of many lands, the entity—after those periods of consecration, those periods of preparation— became an emissary to those of the Indian land, during those periods of the teachings of Saneid.   1294-1

In January of 2002, the Indian Ocean Development and Archaeological Institutes announced the discovery of a 9,500–year–old underwater city in the Gulf of Cambay, off the northwestern coast of India. Scientists located the site in about 120 feet of water early in 2001 during routine monitoring of sea bed pollution levels. Images from an acoustic radar device revealed complex manmade structures running along a five-mile stretch of "paleo" riverbed. Since the structures resembled the oldest known Indian civilization, the *Harappan*, it was originally assumed to date ca. 2500 B.C. However, artifacts removed from the sea bed included a large, cut wooden log that was carbon dated to an astonishing 7500 B.C. Also retrieved were a fossilized jawbone with teeth, pottery, broken pieces of sculpture, and beads.[1,2]

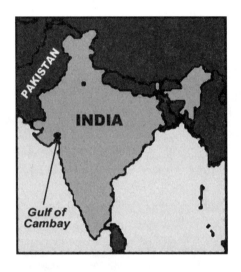

Map of India showing the location of the Gulf of Cambay.

The Harappan civilization is believed to have originated as a small settlement about 3500 B.C. and developed more complex urban centers by about 2500 B.C. However, in 1999, pottery containing a primitive form of writing was discovered at the Harappa site in Pakistan. The pottery was carbon dated to about 3500 B.C., making these artifacts the earliest known examples of writing.[3]

The underwater discovery has shaken the scientific community. Not only is it the oldest found so far in India, it is the oldest group of manmade structures found anywhere in the world. Skeptics have expressed some concern that the project leader may have had political and religious motives for exaggerating the antiquity of the site. Others have simply approached the discovery with caution, awaiting the results of additional research.

CAYCE ON INDIA

For those of us familiar with the Cayce readings regarding the history of humanity, this discovery comes as no surprise. The readings do not focus a great deal on India, but they do indicate that civilization has existed there for at least 50,000 years. In fact, we are told of an Indian ruler by the name of Saad who was involved in a multinational gathering that attempted to rid the world of the dangerous large animals present at that time.[4]

The Cayce readings also tell of a great teacher, named Saneid, who represented India in a compilation of the highest of the worldwide wisdom teachings ca. 10,500 B.C. These spiritual teachings, which were gathered during the time of the priest Ra Ta of Egypt, also came from China, Egypt, Atlantis, the Pyrenees, North and South America, Yucatan, Norway, and "the Carpathian land."[5] As W. H. Church relates in his book, *The Lives of Edgar Cayce*, this effort was part of an attempt by leaders from the five races to perfect the Fourth Root Race, which had just recently (about 12,000 B.C.) been manifested.[6] Although Cayce does not identify India as the location for one specific race, he does identify the area as containing the original projections of both the yellow and white races.[7] According to Cayce, there was much interaction among nations and races in ancient times.

In his book, *Underworld: The Mysterious Origins of Civilization*, Graham Hancock makes a good case for the great antiquity of Indian civilization. Although he does not include the Cayce material in his discussion, some of the information he cites seems to mirror aspects of Cayce's story of Ra Ta and the widespread contact between ancient cultures. First, he notes the similarity of artifacts from India, Egypt, Mesopotamia, and South America, which all depict a hero-type character standing between two lions/leopards while holding them at the throat with each hand. In Sumerian mythology, we know this hero to be the prehistoric Gilgamesh.[8] What makes this of interest in relation to the Cayce readings is that we are told that Ra Ta first entered Egypt with a group from the north who were able to train wild animals, such as bears and leopards, for use in battle.[9] Later, during the period of his banishment in Nubia, Ra Ta was said to have brought to the people in that land a mystical understanding of the creative forces that included the ability to communicate with animals in some manner.[10]

Image of the fish-god from ancient Babylonia—from Ridpath's *History of the World* (1911).

Pictures of Assyrian hero-type character holding lion—from Ridpath's *History of the World* (1911).

A large portion of the India section of Hancock's book covers the legendary seven sages mentioned in ancient Indian texts who lived in a time before the Great Flood. He notes the similarity to the seven sages of Sumerian mythology who were said to be dressed like fish and who emerged from the sea to bring wisdom to all men. He also notes a reference in the Edfu building texts in Egypt to seven sages said to have originally come from an island destroyed by flooding. They are referred to in the texts as the "builder gods" and as the "Lords of Light." Although Hancock does not make the connection, it is interesting that the Cayce readings often describe the Atlanteans as being especially skilled as builders and architects.[11] The readings are also filled with references to a gathering of wisdom teachers around the time of the final destruction of Atlantis. Their purpose was " . . . for the correlating of the truths that were presented by Saneid in the Indian land . . . " [12]

RIG-VEDA: REMNANT OF WISDOM TEACHINGS FROM TIME OF RA TA?

Before that we find the entity was in the Indian land, during those periods when Saneid—one of the great teachers through those experiences—made for the correlating of the general truths with those of other lands. And O that men everywhere would seek to know not their differences, but their unison of thought, their unison of purpose, for their aiding, their helping, their understanding of the needs of others—that all are as One!   1157-1

We could speculate that the oldest known Indian spiritual teachings, the *Rig-veda*, are remnants of the wisdom from the time of Ra Ta. Consisting of over a thousand hymns or lyrical poems, this literature is thought to have been introduced into India by the Aryans, who invaded and conquered the Harappan civilization about 1800 B.C. Archaeologists have been unable to identify a particular culture as Aryan, but often use the term to group together certain languages in the Indo-European family such as Baltic, Armenian, Celtic, Romance, Greek, Albanian, and Slavic. It is generally believed that this group may have originated in Western Asia, possibly near the Carpathian Mountains. If correct, this provides a link with Cayce's story, since he describes Ra Ta as coming from the "the Aryan or the Carpathian land" and later migrating to Egypt.[13] In addition, Cayce refers to an area in the plains of India in 10,500 B.C. as being overrun by "those peoples of the mountains."[14] Since Cayce's view of history contains repeating cycles, perhaps the Aryan invasion, which mainstream Western researchers believe occurred in 1800 B.C., was a replay of such a cycle for India.

The *Rig-veda* forms the basis of the modern Hindu religion of today and is believed to have introduced the concept of a caste system into Indian society. Even more significantly, it is thought to have influenced many other world religions. Perhaps it is simply rooted in principles that originated in a much earlier era and were already present in other cultures as the various religious traditions developed. Of course, the idea of castes and classes conflicts with what the Cayce readings tells us about the wisdom teachings compiled by Ra Ta. However, if the *Rig-veda* does contain spiritual teachings from the time of Ra Ta, it is more likely the result of influences from the older, more peaceful Harappan civilization that predated the so-called "Aryan" invasion of 1800 B.C. Researchers have theorized that the recently discovered 9,500–year–old underwater city is directly related to the Harappan culture, in part because of its distinctive grid–style layout.

There has been much speculation in modern times as to whether the many detailed narratives contained in the *Rig-veda* are actual historical accounts of ancient Indian history. Recent evidence indicates that this may be the case. In 2002, scientists in India reported the discovery, via satellite photography, of a 4,000–year–old river bed which may be the remains of the sacred Saraswati River described in the Vedic hymns as flowing out of the Himalayan Mountains. Most people had assumed that the river was mythical, and its existence has been the subject of much speculation by scientists over the past hundred years. The area identified contains the remains of more than a thousand ancient Harappan culture towns dating back to at least 3000 B.C. One site, Mehrgarh, dates to 6500 B.C. This discovery also supports Cayce and others who claim that India was among several areas of the world with advanced civilizations in existence during the end of the last Ice Age ca. 10,000 B.C.[15]

DISCOVERY OF THE HARAPPAN CIVILIZATION

Evidence for the existence of the Harappan culture was not uncovered until the 1920s and came as a total shock to the archaeological community of the time. Its origins remain a mystery, but the first settle-

Ruins from Harappan settlement—from *Wonders of the Past* (1923).

Harappan decorative seals depicting a unicorn (bottom right), uris (top left), and bison—from *Wonders of the Past* (1923).

Statue of dancing female found at Harappan site— from *Wonders of the Past* (1923).

ments in the rich Indus Valley of northern India have been, so far, traced back to about 3500 B.C. A highly organized, communal, and agricultural civilization, the Harappans occupied cities within an area of 500,000 square miles. The two largest cities were separated by 350 miles. References to them have been found in the Sumerian and Egyptian civiliza–

tions of the third millennium B.C., indicating that they had a wide trade network.

Among the artifacts discovered at these ancient cities are hundreds of decorative seals with highly individualized depictions of animals. One even includes a picture of a unicorn, while another mysteriously contains the likeness of a prehistoric ox called the urus. A sample of pottery, carbon dated to 3500 B.C. and containing a primitive form of writing of unknown origin, was recently discovered at the Harappa site in Pakistan. The script is 200 years older than the Egyptian samples previously considered to be the most ancient.

THE HARAPPAN CULTURE AND THE CAYCE READINGS

Is the Harappan culture a descendant of ancient India during the time of Cayce's Saneid? The 7500 B.C. date for the underwater city would certainly suggest that possibility. In addition, the Harappans are believed to have been highly religious, as evidenced by the large number of ritual, public bathing facilities. Some of their artifacts indicate an emphasis on music and dancing, which could relate to the Temple Beautiful activities of Cayce's Ra Ta period.

Also, the *Rig-veda* describes the Harappans as having dark skin, which could reflect contact with ancient Egyptians even before the time of Ra Ta. In early 2003, Indian scientists announced the results of genetic analysis indicating that early man may have migrated from Africa to India (via the Middle East) around 50,000 years ago. Even more interesting is the fact that there were no genetic differences found between Indians who speak the Indo–European (Aryan) languages and those to the south whose language is called Dravidic. This would indicate that both groups are descended from the same genetic pool possibly as long as 50,000 years ago.[16]

Genetic markers found in residents of both the Gujarat area near the Gulf of Cambay and the Tamil Nadu area of eastern India match those of early man in Africa. Tamil Nadu, like Cambay, has been another area targeted by Graham Hancock for underwater exploration. He claims that a site located off the coast of Poompuhar "could well provide evidence that it was the cradle of civilization." The underwater formations have been studied since the 1980s by India's National Institute of Oceanography and are known to contain several intriguing man-made structures such as well rims and what appear to be horseshoe-shaped buildings. Hancock has received support for his theory from British geologist, Glenn Milne.[17]

In several readings, Cayce identified Saneid as coming from an area "in and around Delhi"[18] and states that, in Ra Ta's time, it was called Deoi.[19] Delhi is located in the Ganges River Valley, which is near the Indus River Valley area, although still somewhat east of any known Harappan settlements. Prehistoric man can be traced back as far as 400,000 years ago in India, but complex civilizations such as the Harappan have not, so far, been discovered near Delhi. However, much of India remains unexcavated, so the jury is still out. For this reason, Indian archaeology continues to be an important area of interest for students of the history of humanity as given in the Cayce readings.

14

America's Mound Builders: Cayce's "Impossible" Chronology

Before that we find the entity was in the land of the present nativity, during those periods when there were the spreadings of those teachings that had come from the lands from which those peoples came that were known as the Lost Tribes, as well as from Atlantis, Yucatan, the Inca, and the land of On[?] [Og?]. They were portions of the entity's people then, in that part of the land now known as the central portion of Ohio, during the early portion of the Mound Builders.

1286-1

In March 2002, we had the pleasure of interviewing and videotaping Edgar Evans Cayce, younger son of Edgar Cayce and first author of *Edgar Cayce on Atlantis* and *Mysteries of Atlantis Revealed*.[1] Fit and mentally sharp at age 84, Edgar Evans was able to lend unique insights into some of the ancient mysteries from the Cayce readings. One of the areas we were especially interested in was the Mound Builders.

Despite living in Alabama and Ohio, two states with huge numbers of ancient Native American mounds, the Cayce family never vis-

The Winterville, Mississippi, mounds are an excellent example of how the later Mound Builders (after A.D. 1000) erected truncated pyramids in patterns. The site is today a state park. Reconstruction by Dee Turman.

ited any mound sites. Edgar Evans recalled a few family talks about mounds, but at the time, there were more important matters in need of attention. Thus little time was given to the mound readings.

The overriding factor in the long-term neglect of Cayce's Mound Builder chronology may be fairly simple. Until recent years, everything Cayce had stated about the Mound Builders was "impossible." That is, the Cayce readings' dates and origins of the Mound Builders were so far from accepted archaeological belief that they "simply couldn't be true." Edgar Evans summarized the problem by saying that, according to Cayce, "the Mound Builders came up from the south," and that his early date of man in the Americas was completely opposed to the commonly accepted archaeological beliefs. "Cayce gave a lot of dates that upset a lot of people," he added.

The majority of Cayce's sixty-eight readings containing information on the Mound Builders were given between the late 1920s and the late 1930s.[2] Until 1927, American archaeologists firmly believed that no one had migrated to the Americas until perhaps 4,000 B.C. But during an archaeological dig in 1927, a spear point was found wedged between bones of an extinct bison killed in 8000 B.C., near Folsom, New Mexico. Then, in 1932, archaeologists found a different type of spear point among mammoth bones near Clovis, New Mexico. The mammoths— enormous elephants with long body hair—had been killed in 9200 B.C. Subsequent excavations found this distinct spear point, called "Clovis," at numerous sites throughout the Americas. The earliest dating of these sites was 9,500 B.C. Thus, beginning in 1932, mainstream archaeology held firm to a 9500 B.C. date (called the "Clovis-First" Barrier) as the first migration into America. These first Americans were believed to be bands of Siberian nomads who had crossed into America at the end of the last Ice Age, when a corridor opened between Siberia and Alaska. They were "Big Game Hunters," supposedly following the herds of mastodon and buffalo moving across the exposed land bridge connecting Asia to the Americas. From 1932 until 1997, American archaeologists contended that the 9500 B.C. "Clovis-First" date was an indisputable fact and that all of the ancestors of Native Americans came from Siberian Asia.[3]

"CLOVIS-FIRST" COLLAPSES

In 1997, a blue ribbon panel of twelve American archaeologists visited an ongoing dig at Monte Verde, Chile, conducted by University of Kentucky archaeologists. The group visited the site to investigate claims that the excavation team had uncovered a pre-Clovis habitation. Most of the panel members were Clovis-First proponents who had long been skeptical of the Monte Verde claims. After an on-site investigation, however, the entire group became convinced that the site had genuinely been occupied at least a thousand years before Clovis. A widely reported press conference was soon held in Chicago for the panel to release their unexpected results.[4] On the very day they officially announced that humans had lived at the site at least a thousand years before Clovis, the ongoing dig found evidence of habitation at the site as long ago as 35,000 B.C.

Archaeologists soon revisited other sites all over the Americas and were incredulous when they found evidence of habitation before Clovis. Amazingly, virtually all previous digs at American sites had stopped when Clovis artifacts were encountered. This was due to a simple flaw in logic that was later pointed out by the archaeologists themselves. Since mainstream archaeology accepted that no evidence of human habitation could exist below the Clovis layer, looking for it was considered to be foolish, a waste of time, and unscientific. But with the Monte Verde finds and the subsequent discovery of pre–Clovis habitation at numerous other sites, suddenly and unexpectedly the Clovis–First barrier had completely collapsed. Humans had been in the Americas well before Clovis, but other discoveries were needed before it would become apparent when these early people came. And one of the biggest surprises to come was where these early Americans originated.

EDGAR CAYCE'S MOUND BUILDER CHRONOLOGY

Although many Cayce readings made it clear that the Americas were already heavily inhabited at the time, Cayce's chronology of the mound-building culture begins about 3000 B.C. A mysterious mound-building group referred to as "remnants of Lost Tribes" arrived at the "southern-most portion of America" by boat.[5] This group remained in this area for a brief but unspecified period and then migrated to the pyramid-building culture located near Mexico City. But all was not well in the Mexico area. Human sacrifice gradually came to be practiced at the pyramid sites in Mexico, including in the Yucatan region, and the descendants of these Lost Tribes decided to escape by returning to America.

According to Cayce, a group of Atlantean descendants was also living in Yucatan at this time. Seeking to flee the spiritual degeneration of human sacrifice, these people began to move north. The Atlantean descendants soon joined up with the descendants of the Lost Tribes and went north to America. They apparently found their way to the Mississippi River area where they began constructing mounds. Their descendants eventually moved into the Ohio River Valley. There they joined with the people already living in the area, where mound building reached its zenith.[6]

ARCHAEOLOGY'S PRE-1997 VIEW OF MOUND BUILDING

Mainstream American archaeology had a generally accepted view of the practice of mound building until several events occurred in 1997. Prior to 1997, however, the following chronology was accepted in the mainstream: Small prototypical burial mounds were built in the Iroquois lands about 3000 B.C. This culture, termed the *Red Paint People*, centered in the northeast and covered their dead in small pits covered with ground hematite. Archaeologists believed that the incredible geometric earthworks and enormous pyramid–shaped mounds (found almost everywhere in America, but centered in Ohio) simply developed over time as a social practice—as a gradual, natural cultural evolution of the then–indigenous people.[7]

In the 1950s, however, the incredible mound and earthwork site of Poverty Point, Louisiana, was fully excavated and surveyed by the American Museum of Natural History. An enormous city had been erected on a tributary of the Mississippi River between the years 2500 B.C. and 1500 B.C. Six artificial earthen embankments, each 50–150 feet in width and 10–15 feet tall, were erected in a semi–octagonal shape about three quarters of a mile long. The embankments were aligned with a huge bird effigy mound, over 70 feet tall and 710 feet by 640 feet in extent. The volume of earth in the embankments would fill the Great Pyramid at Giza 30 times. It is believed that at least 10,000 people lived at Poverty Point. Literally millions of artifacts have been recovered from Poverty Point, and some archaeologists have asserted that this American mound site resulted from a migration from Mexico. The people of Poverty Point then moved up the Mississippi River into Ohio carrying the idea of earthworks and large mounds with them. The thinking now is that, beginning sometime around 1000 B.C., mound building simultaneously emerged all over the eastern half of America because of the Poverty Point influence.[7]

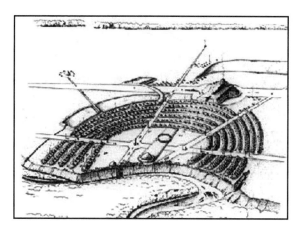

Poverty Point, Louisiana, was the site of America's first effigy mound erected ca. 2500 B.C.-1500 B.C.—from Jon Gipson's *Poverty Point* (1983), State of Louisiana.

THE MYSTERIES OF WATSON BRAKE

In 1993, amateur archaeologists interested state archaeologists in testing a little-known mound site located near Monroe, Louisiana, about fifty miles from Poverty Point. Later, in 1997, scientists announced that Watson Brake, a huge oval embankment with eleven mounds enclosing twenty-two acres, was the oldest known mound site in America. Over

The Watson Brake, Louisiana, mounds were erected between 3400-3000 B.C. by an unknown group of people who remained at the location for only a brief time before moving to parts unknown—from documents of *State of Louisiana, Department of Parks*.

200 carbon dates have come from the site, ranging from 3400 B.C. to 3000 B.C. The site was occupied about 180 years, and then the people from Watson Brake simply disappeared.

Nearly 900 small (1.5-by-2 inch) earthen blocks have been found at Watson Brake and nearby sites associated with it. Many of the blocks recovered from mound excavations at Watson Brake had been carefully arranged into symmetrical cubes formed by the blocks.[8] Archaeologists have no clue as to the nature of these carefully arranged blocks, but they bear an uncanny resemblance to *payim* weights, which were used in Semitic and Hebrew times as counterbalances in trading. In addition, Watson Brake bears a distinctive resemblance to a Semitic encampment.[9]

The finds at Watson Brake were unexpected, but fit Cayce's chronology perfectly. The Louisiana site lies in what could be described as the "southernmost portion of America"—Cayce's term for the first mound site erected by the Lost Tribes.[5] In addition, the site's resemblance to a Semitic encampment and the similarity of the recovered blocks to *payim* weights lend credence to the Lost Tribes' assertion. In addition, the relatively brief habitation of the site and the disappearance of the people of Watson Brake fit Cayce's assertion that these people moved to Mexico. Finally, the emergence of Poverty Point as a mound site erected by people migrating from Mexico completely supports Cayce.

GENETICS RESEARCH CONFIRMING CAYCE'S ANCIENT AMERICA CHRONOLOGY

As described in the earlier chapter on genetics research, an unusual form of genetic testing was conducted on living Native Americans starting in the 1980s. This form of testing, called mitochondrial DNA (mtDNA), could determine the female lineage of individuals who were tested. The tests were also able to show where the ancestors of the tested people came from as well as when they migrated. At the same time, genetic researchers began testing ancient remains that had been recovered from mounds and other sites in America.

By 1996, geneticists believed that all Native Americans' mtDNA was Asian in origin, confirming their Clovis-First idea. But in 1997 an expected form of mtDNA emerged in both living people and in ancient remains. As pointed out earlier, this type of mtDNA (called "Haplogroup X") was not Asian. Since that time, Haplogroup X has turned up in high numbers in remains recovered from mounds in the traditional Iroquois lands as well as other locations. In addition, researchers discovered that Haplogroup X entered northeastern America well before 3000 B.C., but they also found that another group bearing Haplogroup X entered the same lands again in about 1000 B.C. (See further discussion in the chapter on genetics research.) This interesting development perfectly matched Cayce's statement that a combined group of descendants of Lost Tribes and Atlanteans had moved into the Ohio River valleys about that time where they began mound building. In brief, Haplogroup X began to fit the idea that it originated in a no-longer-existing location—Atlantis.

Another series of unexpected genetic findings soon rocked the archaeological world. As geneticists began tracing the mtDNA of both living Native Americans and ancient remains back to their origin, it became clear that not all of the Native American ancestors had come from Siberian Asia. People had come to the Americas from the South Pacific, China, Japan, and also from unknown locations (perhaps Atlantis). All of these locations were specifically mentioned in the Cayce readings. Finally, the dates of migration that emerged from the genetic research didn't fit the Clovis-First idea at all. Groups had entered the Americas several times in ancient times, with the first migration close to 50,000 years ago.

The most commonly accepted archaeological theory, based on both excavations and mitochondrial DNA research conducted on ancient remains, is that three waves of migrations into the Americas probably occurred: 47,000 B.C. to 38,000 B.C.; 28,000 B.C.; and 10,000 B.C. As pointed out in an earlier chapter, Cayce readings stated that migrations to America occurred in three waves: in 50,000 B.C., 28,000 B.C., and 10,000 B.C.—a rather remarkable correlation to the modern genetic findings. Our 2001 book, *Mound Builders*, details all this genetic research as well as Cayce's migration chronology.[2]

WAS CAYCE CORRECT ABOUT THE MOUND BUILDERS?

Watson Brake definitely appears to have been built by a migrating group as a base camp, but the origin of these people is unknown. Fishing was the main activity at the site and it seems more than reasonable to assume they arrived by boats (as Cayce stated). After living there for 180 years, its people disappeared completely. The location, characteristics of the site, its dating (3400–3000 B.C.), and duration of occupation (180 years or so) all fit the Cayce chronology for Lost Tribes arriving at the southernmost portion of America in 3000 B.C. Just as Cayce stated, these people only remained at the site for a relatively few generations before moving on.

The next erection of mounds in America occurred at Poverty Point ca. 2500 B.C. This fact is also consistent with Cayce. The readings cited that it was somewhat later when the Lost Tribe descendants joined with Atlantean descendants from the Yucatan to return to America. Cayce implies that these people went back to America to establish a simpler and more spiritual way of life. According to Cayce, the combined group of Lost Tribes and Atlantean descendants entered America and began mound building in earnest. Gradually the people of Poverty Point appear to have moved north, up the Mississippi River and into the Ohio River Valley. Archaeologists have now accepted that some of the distinct characteristics of the Ohio mound builder cultures were probably influenced by migrations from the south—just as Cayce related nearly eighty years ago.

Incredibly, when Edgar Cayce gave his Mound Builder chronology in various readings, none of it was even remotely close to what archaeology accepted as "truth." But modern excavations and genetic research point to Cayce's chronology as valid. The specificity of Cayce's dates and locations of mound building and migrations appears so close to what we now recognize as historical fact that it seems beyond the realm of coincidence or lucky guesses.

Edgar Evans Cayce told us that "a lot of things that he [Edgar Cayce] said in the 1920s and 1930s were silly then . . . but it's turning out that people were in the places he said they were . . . I can understand how the academic community wouldn't take information from a psychic, but I think they'll make more discoveries in the future that will confirm his information." Indeed!

15

Egyptians in Ancient America: Was Cayce Correct?

Hence the entity was among the daughters of the Law of One, being a priestess of the temple in the Poseidian land *[Atlantis]*; among those that went to the Egyptian land with those peoples the establishing of the associations; also visiting those that established themselves in now the Pyrenees—or the eastern portion of the continental Europe, and those that established themselves in what is now known as a portion of American—in Arizona, New Mexico, Colorado, and those portions of the land.   1144-2

According to the Cayce readings, ancient America was settled by a myriad of people long before Atlanteans fled their remaining islands just prior to 10,000 B.C.[1] People from Mu, earlier Atlantean settlers (ca. 28,000 B.C. and before), people from the South Pacific, and a host of others (coming from "the west") lived throughout the extensive American continents.[2] Modern archaeological excavations and genetic research now indicate that this scenario, once thought to be impossible, is valid.

The idea that cultural migrations to the Americas occurred between the end of the last Ice Age (ca. 9000 B.C.) to the time of Columbus' arrival (A.D. 1492) is referred to as *diffusionism*.

American academic archaeology has long rejected diffusionist theories, asserting that no one, except for perhaps a small Norse group, entered the Americas after the Ice Age until Columbus.

Cayce's readings on ancient visitors and migrations to America were given primarily in the 1930s, well before any evidence started to emerge indicating that such migrational events could be true. For example, in the 1940s a Spanish language book, *Historia de la Nacion Mexicana*, was published by Mariano Cuevas. The English translation of Cuevas' book wasn't available until decades later. Cuevas wrote that Mexican archaeologist M. A. Gonzalez excavated ruins at Acajutla in 1914. Gonzalez uncovered two small statues in the ruins. The statues looked exactly like the Egyptian gods Osiris and Isis.

The Cayce readings include numerous references to Egyptians visiting the southwest region of America. They were primarily involved in establishing ties to religious centers. In the "Four Corners" area, especially around Arizona, New Mexico, and Colorado, Atlanteans joined with a "strayed tribe that came across from Lemuria." A priestess of the "Children of the Law of One" is specifically mentioned who came to Arizona to help establish religious practices.[3] Another reading tells of a temple priestess who had escaped the final destruction of Atlantis by migrating to Egypt. She subsequently visited the Pyrenees and then went to the Atlantean settlements in Arizona, New Mexico, and Colorado.[4] Finally, reading 2540-1 tells of a woman in the southwestern part of America who became a priestess in a community comprised of the Atlantean descendants and others who were practicing Mosaic laws and the teachings of the Law of One. In brief, the time frame covered by these readings indicates that this area was an active religious center from at least 28,000 B.C. to after 3000 B.C.

Possible links to an Egyptian influence have turned up in the American southwest. In the Tortolita Mountains northwest of Tucson, a site known as Zodiac Ridge was first studied in the late 1930s. Zodiac Ridge is a 180-foot rock circle constructed with over 800 stones. It contains alignments to the 18.61-year lunar cycle, the solstices, equinox, and several stars, including the constellation of Orion.[5] While archaeoastronomers believe it was constructed in the early years A.D., nearby are petroglyphs that bear Egyptian-like hieroglyphs.

In 1978, five different cave-like rock shelters came to the attention of Oklahoma's Gloria Farley. Located in the arid panhandle of Oklahoma, the caves' interiors are covered with amazing inscriptions and carvings, many of which appear to be Egyptian. Because of the similarity between the Egyptian god Anubis and carvings of what appears to be Anubis on some of the walls, the caves are called the "Anubis Complex."[6]

Other carvings and inscriptions have been found in the southwest over the years, but none of those that have survived seem to support the existence of a temple complex in the area as related in the Cayce readings. In 1991, however, an archaeological team in Arizona may have discovered the exact temple complex the Cayce readings described. Amazingly, the complex may have been completely looted in 1909 and even documented by newspapers.

AN ANCIENT EGYPTIAN TEMPLE IN ARIZONA?

On April 5, 1909, the *Phoenix Gazette* published a large front-page article titled "Explorations in Grand Canyon." The article reported that an enormous complex of rooms, carved into the side of a sheer canyon wall, had been discovered and entered by a group of archaeologists working for the Smithsonian Institution. The location of the complex was "on government land," and visitors were not welcome or allowed at the secret site. Entrance to the complex of rooms and connecting tunnels was only through a small, hidden cave located over 1000 feet down the sheer cliff of a canyon wall. Nearly 60 feet inside the small cave entrance, tunnels diverged leading to numerous rooms with some being 30 by 40 feet. One room was described as an astonishing 40 by 700 feet. The walls and ceilings of the rooms were expertly chiseled and, while "hundreds of rooms" were supposedly contained in the complex, the article stated that most of the complex had yet to be explored.

Incredible as the description of the massive complex may be, even more incredible is the description of the contents. The catacombs contained artifacts and material clearly Egyptian in origin. Mummies, various idols and images, copper, gold, and other metallic artifacts, utensils, and advanced forms of pottery were found along with stone tablets bearing hieroglyphic writings. Several specific individuals were named in the newspaper article including G. E. Kincaid and Professor S. A. Jordan (supposedly of the Smithsonian).

Modern archaeologists contend that the newspaper article was a hoax and that the complex never existed. In fact, it is known that many newspapers during this era did publish sensationalized fictional articles. In addition, the Smithsonian has established a standard reply to the many inquiries it receives about the 1909 article: "The Smithsonian's Department of Anthropology has searched its files without finding any mention of a Professor Jordan, Kincaid, or a lost Egyptian civilization in Arizona."

WAS THIS TEMPLE REDISCOVERED IN 1991?

In *Mound Builders*, the authors of the present book described a little-known discovery made in 1991 near the Little Colorado River, west of Springerville, Arizona.[7] The first public acknowledgment of the find was made in the *Arizona Daily Sun* on April 27, 1991. This occurred at the Society of American Archaeology Annual Conference in New Orleans after three archaeologists made a report on their astonishing find. While working at what is now the Arizona-operated Casa Malpais archaeological park, the three archaeologists spotted what seemed to be a small cave opening, hidden down the face of a sheer canyon wall. After rappelling down the wall, a small cave opening was confirmed, and they slowly crawled into it. Deep inside the small opening, tunnels were discovered, leading to what archaeologists concede is perhaps the most unique archaeological find in all of the Americas. In fact, there has never been anything similar *ever* found in the Americas.

"Catacombs" of dozens of rooms were discovered interconnected by tunnels enclosed in an area described in the archaeological reports as an astonishing "three to four acres in extent." The rooms had been carefully carved, with ceilings as high as fifty feet. Some of the rooms were over a hundred feet long. No artifacts have been described from the closely guarded, secret catacombs. However, archaeologists speculate that the catacomb of rooms was probably a Mogollon burial complex simply because of its proximity to a known Mogollon site. While this conclusion is comforting to archaeologists, the primary problem with this interpretation is simple and acknowledged by archaeologists: Nothing like this site has *ever* been found.

Our correspondence with the archaeologists who made the discovery only deepened the mystery. No pictures from the site are available for public view, and artifacts possibly discovered in the catacombs are not discussed. Contractual agreements restrict the discovering archaeologists from providing any additional information. The nearby Mogollon ruins at Casa Malpais are available for tour, but entrance into the catacomb complex is strictly forbidden and is kept secret. The reasoning behind the secrecy is understandable. First, entrance to the Casa Malpais catacomb complex is extremely dangerous. Secondly, if the location becomes known, looters and vandals most certainly will leave their destructive mark at the site. However, lack of information about possible artifacts is curious.

ARE THE 1909 AND 1991 COMPLEXES ONE AND THE SAME?

In *Mound Builders*, we speculated that Casa Malpais might, in fact, be the same site discussed in the 1909 newspaper article. It is very probable that the individuals interviewed for the 1909 article were not who they said they were—just as the Smithsonian has officially stated. Kincaid and Jordan may have stated that they were from the Smithsonian to give an impression of authority, when they were actually just looters. The use of a pseudonym certainly points to this conclusion. Giving a false location of the site would also fit this idea. Giving the descriptions of the artifacts to the newspaper reporter may have become necessary for the perpetrators, especially if someone had seen a few artifacts and described them to the newspaper. We may never know the facts, but the descriptions of the site entrance and its interior in the 1909 newspaper article and the 1991 archaeologists' report are nearly identical.

The Arizona location of Casa Malpais, only twenty miles from New Mexico, is intriguing because it clearly fits the Cayce readings' location given for the early settlement of groups devoted to practicing Mosaic laws and the Law of One. In addition, with the Cayce readings telling of an Egyptian priestess visiting this site and the probable establishment of a temple there (including one in "Canyon Island"), we are led to the possibility that Egyptian-like religious artifacts and mummies could have been placed there.[8] This is precisely what the 1909 article stated was found in the complex.

However, it is simply not known whether the 1909 descriptions of the artifacts removed from the site are accurate. What is certain, however, is that a gigantic, unique complex of mysterious rooms carved from rock exists inside a canyon wall in Arizona. The existence of it baffles archaeologists, and the contents within it apparently create an unsettling feeling in the archaeological community.

16

Odin:
Norse God or King?

. . . the entity was of a peoples who were drawn to the
ideas and ideals prompted from the great Odin, who
brought a message as to the relationships of individuals
with the First Cause . . .   1468-6

Norse mythology has been passed
down for over a thousand years in the Eddic
poems, which are still preserved in thirteenth-
century Icelandic manuscripts. The story told
in these myths describes the "beginning" as a
time when the world was dominated by the
extremes of ice and fire. From the void between
these two extremes, life originated. As the ice
in the world melted, several creatures emerged.
An offspring of some of these creatures was
Odin, who later became the chief of all the
gods, for he was the greatest among them.

Although the story of Odin has long been
assumed to be totally mythological, the sagas
relate an astonishing amount of detail. They tell
that Odin was the son of Bestla (daughter of
Jotun) and Bor (son of Bure). Odin was a sage
and magician who became king after leading a
successful revolt with his brothers against the
leader Ymer. As his myth evolved over time,
Odin was elevated to the status of a god, who
breathed life into the first man and woman.

Odin (seated) is usually depicted as an actual person. Others depicted are Thor, Tyr, and Loke—from *The Iconographic Encyclopaedia of Science, Literature, and Art* **(1851).**

THE CULT OF ODIN

It is believed by scholars that the Odin "cult" was spread from western Germany to Scandinavia only a few centuries before the legends were recorded. Medieval Christian historians are known to have altered elements of Norse mythology, so the stories told by various texts vary somewhat.

Odin was worshipped under different names throughout northern Europe. The Germans called him Wotan, and the English, Woden. The influence of the cult of Odin was so profound that the days of the week were named after him and his family. Human sacrifice became an important part of the cult, and texts dated as early as the ninth century describe how sacrificial victims were ceremoniously killed. While his exploits are rendered in meticulous detail by the ancient manuscripts, few archaeologists have ever given credence to the idea that Odin may have been a real person in history.

Snorre Sturluson's thirteenth-century sagas recorded the most detailed accounts of Odin. Odin himself supposedly wrote a series of poetic manuscripts available today under the title *The Elder* or *Poetic Edda*.[1] The sagas and poems relate that Odin's spear, named *Grungir*, never missed and that he was able to shoot ten arrows at a time from his bow. He had a magic ring (*Draupnir*), which created nine duplicates of itself. The stories associated with Odin are believed to have been the inspiration for J. R. R. Tolkien's *Lord of the Rings* books.

ODIN IN THE CAYCE READINGS

Four Cayce readings discuss Odin, and, in all of them, he is treated as a real person.

- In a follow-up life reading, Cayce explained that a female who had been born in the Norse lands was a follower of the "ideas and ideals prompted from the great Odin," especially relating to supernatural events.[2]
- In another life reading, a man was told he had been Odin. Cayce related that he and others journeyed to the "north woods" of the United States from the Norse lands. [3]
- In a third reading, Cayce told a man that he had been a Norse voyager to Vinland, and he suggested that the man could benefit from a study of Odin.[4]
- In a fourth reading, Cayce told a woman that she had been the companion of the leader of the Norse, following the Norse invasions of Holland and Germany. Cayce called the Norse leader Olson Odin.[5] Whether this reading refers to the mythical Odin is unknown, but it is unlikely.

In depicting Odin as a genuine king in history, Cayce definitely went against the historical and archaeological community of his time. However, new evidence shows that Odin may have actually existed, just as the Cayce readings stated.

WAS ODIN A REAL PERSON?

Thor Heyerdahl is famous for his expeditions tracing early civilizations, most notably his Kon Tiki expedition of 1947, when he sailed in a reed boat from Peru to Polynesia. In 2001, at eighty-six years of age, Heyerdahl turned his attention to the legend of Odin and the origins of the Scandinavian people. (Heyerdahl died in 2002 at the age of eighty-seven.)

In 1994, he visited Azerbaijan to view boat petroglyphs (rock carvings) in the ancient caves of Gobustan, not far from Baku. In a 1995 issue of *Azerbaijan International*, Heyerdahl revealed that he believed the ancient Scandinavians migrated from Azerbaijan. A large seafaring civilization was centered there on an inland sea in ancient times. In fact, Heyerdahl asserted that the area near Azerbaijan and Turkey was the homeland of the Caucasians who populated Europe in very early times. Interestingly, the Cayce readings state that the Caucasian race first appeared in that same area.[6]

Heyerdahl found identical drawings of ancient boats in caves at Gobustan and in Scandinavia. Also in Gobustan, Russian archaeologists led him to Roman inscriptions telling of the entrance of Roman troops into the area in A.D. 97. This event became an important clue in Heyerdahl's last quest.

Sturluson's thirteenth-century text related that Odin and his people migrated to Norway from a land called *Aser* in order to avoid conflict with the advancing Romans. The ancient descriptions of Aser perfectly matched the Sea of Azov in southern Russia, east of the Black Sea. But Heyerdahl needed physical evidence that the area was Odin's Aser.

In the past few years, convincing evidence supporting Heyerdahl's idea emerged in archaeological digs conducted by Scandinavian and Russian archaeologists near the Dan River at Azov in Azerbaijan. Based on the details given in Snorre's Saga, Heyerdahl was led to a specific location where he believed Odin's land of Aser could be found. At that spot, ancient Viking artifacts were uncovered in a series of excavations. Metal belt holders, rings, and armbands dated from A.D. 100-200 were found that exactly matched objects unearthed in Scandinavia. To

Heyerdahl, this was proof that Azov was the legendary Aser, the home of Odin.

ODIN'S DEPARTURE FROM ASER/AZOV

Heyerdahl also noted that the actual historical lineage of Norse kings recounted in the first *Sagas* began in A.D. 800, and that thirty-one generations passed between Odin and the first recorded historical king. Anthropologists count an average of twenty-five years for each ruling generation of a king, so if he actually existed, Odin most likely lived during the first century. This dating matched the archaeological finds of Viking artifacts at Azov and the nearby Roman inscriptions dated to A.D. 97.

The Chinese Academy of Sciences then reported the discovery of blond-haired mummies in the Karim Desert, located in the heart of China. Carbon dating placed the burials at 1800–1500 B.C. Chinese archaeologists determined that the mummies were not Mongoloid and suspected that they were Vikings. The cloth that had been uncovered with the mummies was sent to the United States, where it was found to be typical of that of the Celts of Ireland. Since the distinctive color and texture of ancient Celtic cloth was Scythian, Heyerdahl concluded that there were early migrations to China by Caucasians (Vikings) from the Azov area.

According to Heyerdahl, the historical Odin was the chief of the Aesir tribe living in the Azov area during the first century. When Roman expansion posed a threat late in the first century, they left the region. With his migrating tribe, Odin conquered Russia, Germany, Denmark, and Norway, finally arriving in Sweden in about A.D. 100. Sweden's King Gylfi gave Odin half of his realm to maintain peace. In Sweden, Odin founded the city of Sigtuna. His later descendents—the Saxons Hengist and Horsa—later conquered Britain.

Heyerdahl released his findings in a late 2001 book, *The Hunt for Odin*. He expressed certainty that Odin was a real king who went to Sweden from Azov with his followers in A.D. 100, after the Romans invaded.

MYTHOLOGY AND HISTORY

Heyerdahl asserted that what we take for imagination or "mythology" in these ancient texts is an actual account of historical events. He
spent his life proving that legends and myths from all parts of the world
were not just possible, but represented genuine history. While most
archaeologists discount mythology, other great thinkers have seen truth
relayed in the stories, For example, in his classic 1960 book, *Answer to Job*,
the famous psychologist Carl Jung observed that "all myths have a basis
in reality." But in a 2001 *Reuter's* press release on his find, Heyerdahl
stated that he doubted that his book and the archaeological finds would
convince the hard-core archaeologists.

Thor Heyerdahl was certainly one of the most influential anthropological explorers of our time. His expeditions have shown that Cayce's
stories of ancient migrations by seafaring civilizations aren't just possible, they are probable. This latest find is yet another significant addition to the growing body of evidence supporting the Cayce readings'
account of the ancient world.

17

The Tower of Babel: An Atlantean Legend?

Yet man in his greed, in his own selfishness, has set himself so oft at naught by the very foolishness of his own wisdom . . . And this expression came into such measures that there arose the periods when man came as *one* and said, "We will *build* . . . And then came the diversity of tongues and confusion arose. For the very selfishness of man had brought this confusion, this defiance to a God of love, of mercy, of patience. . . .

262-96

According to Genesis (11:1–9), the king of Babel (in Chaldea) was a proud and powerful warrior named Nimrod, a great grandson of Noah, from the line of Ham and Cush. The descendants of Noah had become so numerous that it was decided that a high tower should be built as an expression of earthly power and to create unity among the group. God became concerned that if the people could come together to create such a great work, " . . . nothing will later stop them from doing whatever they presume to do." Since all of the people in the world spoke the same language, God decided to "confuse their language" and scatter them "all over the earth."

The biblical Tower of Babel has sparked the imaginations of archaeologists for over two centuries, and yet its existence remains shrouded in mystery. It is unclear whether the story is allegorical or historical, and the scientific evidence appears to point both ways. Cayce mentions it in several readings primarily to point out the folly of depending solely on our human abilities. But even the readings are unclear as to whether or not there was a single event centered on a particular building.

Ziggurat or Mound of Birs-Nimrod—from G. Barton's *Archaeology and the Bible* **(1916).**

Early picture of the Ziggurat of Ur in Iraq—from G. Barton's *Archaeology and the Bible* **(1916).**

WAS THERE AN ACTUAL TOWER OF BABEL?

One problem in trying to verify this story is that Bible chronology is not an exact science. According to the Sumerian creation story called *The Epic of Gilgamesh*, a deluge resembling Noah's flood occurred sometime between 3400 B.C. and 2900 B.C. Bible scholars, however, date it to either 2239 B.C. (in the Masoretic Hebrew version) or 3100 B.C. (in the Greek and Samaritan versions).[1] Given these dates, archaeologists believe that ancient temple buildings (called *ziggurats,* meaning "high point") discovered in present-day Iraq may be examples of the Tower of Babel. The Sumerians and Akkadians, who were ancestors of the Babylonians, constructed them using mud brick during the third millennium B.C. (See discussion in the chapter on the oldest pyramids.) However, the identification of an actual Tower of Babel has not, as yet, been confirmed.[2]

One of these ancient structures, the Ziggurat of Ur, received worldwide attention during both the 1991 and 2003 Gulf Wars. In the first of these, Saddam Hussein surrounded the site with military units that subsequently drew U.S. mortar fire that damaged one of the outer walls. In early 2003, the site was spared from bomb damage. However, antiquities experts around the world pleaded for increased security to protect the monument from potential looting. One scholar was quoted as saying, "The royal tombs of Ur are the richest source of art and archaeology in the Middle East after the temple of Tutankhamen."[3]

There are two ziggurats in particular that are often cited as possible candidates for the biblical Tower of Babel. Nebuchadnezzar rebuilt both during the fifth century B.C. upon the ruins of older structures. And more significantly, both were found near the historical city of Babylon.[4] According to the *Jewish Encyclopedia,* the names Babylon and Babel are both derived from the ancient Semitic word *babili,* which means "the gate of god" or "the gate of Belus," the mythical founder of Babylon. Belus (also Bel or Baal) is sometimes used as a title, meaning "lord" or "master" and may have referred to King Nimrod.

One of these ziggurats is within the ruins of the city of Babylon, which is located on the east bank of the Euphrates River, seventy miles south of modern Baghdad in Iraq. It was named "The House whose top is the Heavens" by Nebuchadnezzar and was visited by the historian Herodotus in 460 B.C. Xerxes later destroyed it during the Persian conquest. Some scholars point to this tower as the most likely Tower of Babel, since the Bible specifies that both a city and a tower were built. The other candidate for the Tower of Babel, called Birs-Nimrud, is located at Borsippa, seven miles southwest of Babylon.

Originally, both ziggurats probably had seven levels, which were colored and dedicated to particular planets. The colors were black (Saturn), white (Venus), orange (Jupiter), blue (Mercury), scarlet (Mars), silver, (Moon), and gold (Sun). The one in Babylon had a spiral staircase on the outer and inner walls[5]

Procession of Bel-Nimrod— from Ridpath's *History of the World* (1911).

Did Nimrod Exist?

As with many of the early biblical characters, such as Noah and Abraham, hard archaeological evidence for the existence of Nimrod is scant. His name does appear in many Middle Eastern legends as well as in the histories of Josephus. The name Nimrod is interpreted in Rabbinical literature as "he who made all the people rebellious against God." He is considered to have introduced both the eating of meat and the waging of war. His name is mentioned in the Old Testament spanning a period of five hundred years. However, some scholars believe that there were two Nimrods. Others believe that Nimrod was not an individual, but an entire tribe of people.[6]

One story in Hebrew mythology tells that Nimrod inherited from his father Cush the garment Adam wore when he was expelled from the Garden of Eden. It had been passed down to Noah and was stolen by his son Ham. When Nimrod wore the garment, it gave him great power and made him invincible so that he was worshipped as a god by the peoples of all the earth. This, in turn, "made men forget the love and worship of the true God, the Creator of the Universe."[7]

After the fall of the Tower of Babel, according to the Bible, Nimrod became a nemesis of Abraham. Toward the end of Nimrod's life, Hebrew legend states that an angel appeared to him and asked him to repent. He refused and, while attempting to gather an army to wage battle with God, was struck down by a tiny insect that had crawled through his nose and into his brain. After forty years of suffering and pain, he died. Known as the original "mighty hunter" for his great size and power, he is associated with the constellation Orion where Hebrew mythology states that he was bound as a punishment for building the tower.[8]

DID A SINGLE LANGUAGE EXIST?

It is possible that there may have been a common language among Semitic peoples in the immediate area, but there is no evidence for a single worldwide language during the third millennium B.C. Hebrew tradition states that the language spoken by the people at Babel was a form of ancient Hebrew. However, in the Moslem version of this story, the common language is said to have been of Assyrian origin.[9]

WERE THE PEOPLE OF BABEL "SCATTERED OVER ALL THE EARTH"?

As discussed in previous chapters, genetic and archaeological evidence is pointing more and more to pre-Columbian transoceanic contact between the Old and New Worlds. One Cayce reading states that, in 3000 B.C., "lost tribes" arrived by boat in North America and eventually migrated to Central Mexico near present-day Mexico City. Earlier in the reading, Cayce describes a "mosaic influence," which many have interpreted to mean Hebrew.[10] This has created some confusion, since "Lost Tribes" is a term normally reserved for the ten tribes of Israel who were conquered by the Assyrians about 600 B.C. However, the *Book of Mormon* tells of a group of monotheistic, Hebrew-like Semitic peoples that migrated to Central America as a result of the fall of the Tower of Babel. Although still controversial, archaeologist John Sorensen and others are finding much evidence to support this possibility.[11]

WAS THE TOWER BUILT BY CAYCE'S SONS OF BELIAL?

Robert Krajenke, in his series, *Edgar Cayce's Story of the Old Testament*, argues that the Book of Genesis is a highly compressed version of Cayce's history of humanity, which contains a repeating cycle of creation, sin, and purification, as discussed in an earlier chapter. Over a period spanning millions of years, souls that were once united with God had become trapped in physical bodies. According to the readings, there were two main groups of souls in Atlantis prior to the Flood. One group was more spiritually conscious (the Sons of the Law of One), while the other was focused on power, pleasure, and material gain (the Sons of Baal or Belial). If, as Cayce says, Noah's flood caused one of the three destructions of Atlantis, then his story of the mighty and rebellious Atlanteans dispersing to various locations may in fact be contained in the story of Babel.[12]

Although Cayce does not mention the name Nimrod in the readings, Rabbinical literature describes him allegorically as the "prototype of a rebellious people."[13] Perhaps the story simply encapsulates the escapades of the Sons of Belial over the millennia. One Hebrew legend says that Nimrod built the Tower of Babel and at its apex placed a gigantic gem upon which, "sitting in divine state, he exacted universal homage."[14] This gemstone must have been enormous and is reminiscent of the great firestone crystal that was installed under the dome in Atlantis, according to Cayce.[15] Other Hebrew myths refer to a battle between

Nimrod's Sons of Ham and the more holy Sons of Japheth.[16]

ARE WE STILL FEELING THE IMPACT OF BABEL TODAY?

Regardless of whether the Tower of Babel is fact or allegory, it contains a very powerful message. No matter how advanced we think we are, we can only go so far using our earthly or human abilities. In one reading, Cayce tells us specifically that the Tower was an attempt to provide a place of safety in the event of another flood.[17] Instead of seeking to live in harmony with the Creative Forces, however, Nimrod and his followers believed they could defy God and yet be protected from any consequences. Through their attempt to maintain unity and security, they actually created the opposite effect, since God divided them into nations (languages) and scattered them over the earth.

As we look at world conditions today, it is obvious that we are still struggling to overcome the challenges created by this dispersion into different languages and cultures. The lesson of the Tower of Babel is that anything we try to accomplish without the cooperation of God is destined to end up in utter confusion. As Cayce puts it, "Know that true knowledge is God . . . " and that our ultimate purpose on earth is to grow to become companions with the Creator.[18]

18

Sodom and Gomorrah: Legend or History?

As has been so oft given, all places—as Egypt, or Sodom or the Crucifixion, or the Lord—are conditions, circumstances, experiences, as well as individual places . . . Thus these to the people represent—Egypt, the release from bondage, Gomorrah, as a reckoning with sin—as the Lord was crucified there.   281-33

For many years, the scientific community looked upon the biblical story of Sodom and Gomorrah as nothing more than a legend. Some, however, have been intrigued by the fact that references to the destruction of these ancient cities are found not only in the book of Genesis, but also in the books of Deuteronomy, Isaiah, Jeremiah, and, most significantly, in several books of the New Testament. The historian Josephus recounted the story, and it is also found in the Moslem *Qur'an*. Archaeological discoveries near the Dead Sea seem to provide confirmation that the events depicted in Genesis regarding the demise of these cities actually occurred just as written. The Cayce readings also treat the destruction of Sodom and Gomorrah as an actual event, since none other than Edgar Cayce himself was told that he had been one of the "angels" sent to warn Abraham and Lot.

Lot fleeing Sodom and Gomorrah as his wife looks back—from Gustave Dore (1875).

Stone formation at Dead Sea traditionally known as "Lot's wife"—from Art Today.

WHAT THE BIBLE TELLS US

In Genesis 18, we are told that three men visit the Hebrew Patriarch Abraham. We later learn that one of them is "the Lord," who, among

other things, tells Abraham that the sinful cities of Sodom and
Gomorrah must be destroyed. Since Abraham's relative Lot and his family reside in Sodom, Abraham pleads with the Lord to spare the cities
for the sake of the "righteous" men living there. Meanwhile, the other
two men leave for Sodom, where they are to warn Lot and his family of
the coming destruction and help them escape. It is at this point in the
story that the two men are referred to as angels.

The evil residents of Sodom attempt to persuade Lot to hand over
the angels to them, but Lot offers them his daughters instead. As they
begin to overpower Lot, the angels cause them to become blind. The
angels then warn Lot to gather his family and leave. Some members of
Lot's family refuse to comply, and even Lot is reluctant. Eventually, the
angels find it necessary to take Lot, his wife, and two daughters by the
hand in order to lead them out of the city.

Lot is then instructed to travel to the mountains and not to look
back. However, he pleads to be allowed to go to a nearby smaller city
named Zoar, which is consequently spared from destruction. Then "the
Lord rained upon Sodom and upon Gomorrah brimstone and fire from
the Lord out of heaven." (Gen. 19:24) Lot's wife, disobeying instructions,
looks back and becomes "a pillar of salt." (Gen. 19:26) Afterwards,
Abraham looks out over the plains from some special vantage point
and sees nothing but smoke where the cities were located. Confirmation of the extent of the destruction caused by this event is found in the
New Testament, in the words of Jesus to the Pharisees: "But the same
day that Lot went out of Sodom it rained fire and brimstone from
heaven, and destroyed them all." (Luke 17:28)

WHAT WAS THE SIN OF SODOM?

Although most conservative Christian groups have assumed that the
sin of Sodom and Gomorrah was sexually related, many ancient Hebrew texts identify the sin as involving greed, theft, and mistreatment
of outsiders. For example, one story tells of a law passed in Sodom
requiring that all nonresidents be expelled and "poor men seeking food
never to receive a piece of bread."[1] In another story we are told of a
kindhearted resident of Sodom who was executed for providing food

and shelter to a visitor. It seems that strangers entering the city were routinely stripped of their clothing and belongings before being ceremoniously thrown out. People were very prosperous, yet hoarded their wealth. Often they carefully hid their valuables in secret places. Another version of the story tells of residents who would attempt to locate these places by asking the owner to store a pitcher of strong-smelling balsam for them for safekeeping. They would then use dogs to help them relocate the balsam so that they could steal the owner's things. The society was described as having much order and many laws so that it was actually quite peaceful. However, as one source put it, these laws were "perverted" to favor the rich and powerful and to prohibit the practice of charity.[2]

THE SEARCH FOR SODOM AND GOMORRAH

Until the late 1960s, archaeologists rejected the idea that the story of Sodom and Gomorrah could be anything more than a morality tale. Attempts to locate hard evidence for the existence of the five "cities of the plains" (described in Genesis 10:19 as being east of the Jordan River) were unsuccessful. The most well-known of these early researchers, W. F. Albright, concluded that Sodom and Gomorrah had been submerged into the Dead Sea. The discovery of ancient tree growth under the southern portion of the Dead Sea in 1960 seemed to confirm that finding.[3]

Then from 1965 to 1973, archaeologists made a series of startling discoveries while excavating a great fortress in the area called Bab edh-Dhra. The site had been discovered originally by Albright, who, upon examining seven fallen monoliths found there, concluded that it had simply been a place of religious pilgrimage. By 1973, however, researchers had determined that Bab edh-Dhra had actually been a large, highly organized city, with an elaborate cemetery that appeared to contain the remains of over a half million people. Similar findings were made at the nearby sites of Feifa, Numeira, Safi, and Khanazir. All five sites were located on the high points of the plains and dated to the period 3000 B.C.–2000 B.C. Each city overlooked one of the five *wadis*, or river valleys, that connect with the Dead Sea. Archaeologists now believe that

Bab ehd-Dhra was most likely Sodom, Numeira was Gomorrah, and
Safi was Zoar.[4]

EVIDENCE OF A DECADENT LIFESTYLE

Even more interesting, the evidence uncovered at the sites indicated
that the residents might have led a decadent lifestyle, as depicted in the
Bible. For example, they were unusual in that they neither lived in, nor
buried their dead in, family groups, but instead practiced some sort of
communal living. They were also very prosperous, of healthy stature,
and appeared to have lived primarily in an open area of the city rather

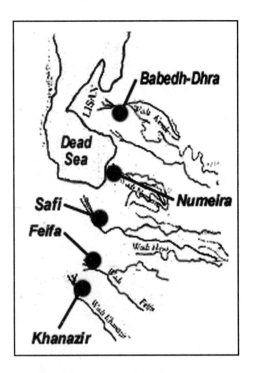

**Locations of biblical cities of Sodom (Bab
ehd-Dhra), Gomorrah (Numeira) and
Zoar (Safi) near the Dead Sea—by G.
Little.**

than in separate buildings. It is believed that the residents were wealthy traders, craftsmen, and herders (like Lot), and that they had a significant leisure class. Grave artifacts included figurines that indicated the presence of fertility worship.

The most compelling discovery was that there had been widespread burning at three of the cities, which were covered by a thick layer of ash several feet deep. In addition, Dr. Bryant Wood determined that the fire most likely began on the roofs of the various buildings. But what could cause this type of fire? Scientists have long known that the area contains active fault lines. Major earthquakes could have caused the eruption of highly flammable balls of tar (asphalt) that could have easily been ignited by lightning or some other means. Wood and others have speculated that this would fit the Bible's assertion that it "rained fire and brimstone from heaven," which would certainly have caused catastrophic destruction.[5]

THEORIES OF ANCIENT NUCLEAR EXPLOSION

Some authors have proposed that the destruction of Sodom and Gomorrah was the result of an ancient nuclear explosion.[6,7] This is based primarily on the discovery of sand at ancient levels of the strata which had been fused into glass by exposure to extreme heat. Modern nuclear testing has created the same sort of geological anomaly. Some examples, such as the three glass-lined craters discovered by St. John Philby in 1932[7] in the empty quarter of southern Saudi Arabia, have been determined to be the result of meteoric impact.[8] Others, such as the beautiful glass uncovered in the Libyan desert area of Western Egypt, have been the subject of some controversy since craters cannot be definitively identified. A report given at a recent meeting of the Annual Meteoritical Society provided results of a chemical analysis, which seems to confirm that the glass was most likely produced by meteoric impact. The researchers were also able to rule out an above-ground blast such as occurred in Tunguska, Siberia, in 1908.[10]

Cayce on the Lesson of Sodom and Gomorrah

As indicated in the quote at the beginning of this article, Cayce viewed the story of Sodom and Gomorrah as both an allegory and an actual event. In one reading, he was asked to explain the warning given to Lot's wife to "not look back." As Cayce explained, "Lot's wife looked upon that left as longing for those satisfying elements that made for the carnal, rather than the spiritual life." Robert Krajenke, in *Edgar Cayce's Story of the Old Testament*, notes that Lot was similarly tempted, since he initially refused to go with the angel to the mountaintop.[11]

One of the most interesting connections to this story occurred in a dream Cayce had in 1932, in which he was escaping the rain of fire with Lot and his wife. A subsequent reading given to interpret the dream informed Cayce that in a past life he had been one of the angels sent to warn Lot. Furthermore, he was told that the dream was given to him to point out that he was now faced with a decision much like that of Lot when he was on the mountaintop. At this time, a discouraged Cayce was considering leaving Virginia Beach because of the loss of his hospital and financial support. As the reading indicated, Virginia Beach was the place (recommended by the readings) most conducive to his work. To leave would show a lack of faith and would in effect be "looking back."[12]

Cayce also used this story to encourage people to believe in the power of prayer. Some of these readings were directed at concerns about the Second World War, and others related to Cayce's prophecies regarding future destructive earth changes. "And as of old, the prayers of ten may save a city; the prayers of twenty-five may save a nation—as the prayers and activities of *one* may!"[13] In another reading Cayce made a statement relevant to the tragedies of September 11, 2001, in that he indicated that we have not only *power* through prayer, but an *obligation* to pray for our neighbors throughout the world: "He who has faltered; he who has fallen even by the way. *He* is thine neighbor, and thou must answer for him!"[14] In other words, we are all in this together, and our prayers for others ultimately affect us as well.

19

The Mysterious Oracle Stones: The Urim and Thummim

And thou shalt put in the breastplate of judgment the Urim and the Thummim; and they shall be upon Aaron's heart, when he goeth in before the Lord: and Aaron shall bear the judgment of the children of Israel upon his heart before the Lord continually.

Exod. 28:30

As He has spoken through prophet, through sage, through Urim, through Thummim, through dream, through vision, since man has been in materiality or in matter, so may the spirit of truth still give expression to those that seek His face, and to find expression of same among their fellow man.   338-3

The Hebrew words *Urim* and *Thummim* have been translated to mean "the Light [revelation] and the Truth [perfection]." The Urim and Thummim were special tools for attunement prescribed by Jehovah through Moses for use by Aaron at the time of the establishment of the priesthood of the Levites. The scripture is clear that they were to be worn underneath the jeweled breastplate of the high priest, next to his heart. However, beyond that bit of infor-

mation, their origins and composition are a mystery. Most Bible scholars have concluded that they were very likely used as a type of oracle to
receive Divine Guidance.[1] The Cayce readings agree and make a point
of emphasizing that the Urim and Thummim did not actually contain
the power itself, but were merely a means of channeling the Creative
Forces.[2] In fact, Cayce put the use of these tools on the same level as
obtaining guidance and attunement through dreams, meditation, and
intuition or psychic perception.[3]

**The Breastplate of the Hebrew
High Priest. The Urim and
Thummim were placed next to
the heart, behind this bejeweled
plate as part of the "priestly
dress"—from *The Jewish Encyclopedia* (1905).**

ANCIENT ORIGINS OF THE URIM AND THUMMIM

Some biblical experts speculate that the Urim and Thummim were stones made of lapis lazuli.[4] If so, this would parallel Cayce's identification of lapis as a stone that may be used to enhance psychic ability. Cayce stated that those who were sensitive enough could actually "hear those vibrations giving off, or the singing or talking stones . . . "[5]

The Hebrew historian Josephus describes the Urim and Thummim that gave off a brilliant light to signify a favorable answer to questions posed by the priest. Other historians speculate that they were gems engraved with the name of Jehovah. The priest used the stones to concentrate and become focused in order to receive some prophetic revelation. But the most interesting connection is that Josephus indicates that the stones were in existence *prior* to the time of Moses. In fact, some scholars have traced their origins to the Egyptian culture, which was known to use the lapis lazuli to represent the virtues of truth and revelation. Egyptian judges wore the stone over their breasts, suspended by a gold chain, and used them to touch the lips of acquitted persons.[6] The Urim and Thummim also seem to be similar to the "Tablets of Destiny" described in ancient Assyrian/Babylonian texts. These were also stones worn as a breastplate and used only "by those gods who, in some way, were considered the messengers and mediators between other gods and mankind."[7]

Other historians believe the stones represent an attempt to renew an older ritual in which the ancient Semitic Patriarchs used another mysterious ancient form called the "Teraphim." As with the Urim and Thummim, scholars differ on the true nature of the Teraphim. One theory is that the Teraphim was "an image made by astrologers at a certain time and under the influence of certain stars which caused it to speak." There seems to be agreement that the Teraphim's power was misused. It appears to have devolved into the worship of graven images, a practice often condemned in the Old Testament. In fact, it is believed that the Teraphim, which predated the Urim and Thummim, was an attempt to create a substitute for an earlier version of the Urim and Thummim, again indicating that their origin is indeed quite ancient.[8]

Example of a *Mazzebah* (Phoenician) or sacred stone often erected by Semitic peoples during the time of the biblical Patriarchs—from *The Jewish Encyclopedia* (1905).

Urim and Thummim: Remnant of Atlantean Firestone?

Could the Urim and the Thummim be a form of the Atlantean firestone preserved over time by the descendants of the Sons of the Law of One? Cayce stated that, although the firestone eventually was used as a power-producing tool, its original purpose was to aid in spiritual communication: " . . . [The firestone] was in the form of a six-sided figure, in which the light appeared as the means of communication between infinity and the finite . . . "[9]

In fact, the Cayce readings say, "stones that are circular, that were of the magnetized influence" were brought to the Yucatan by Atlantean immigrants to allow the "angels of light" to communicate with the people.[10] He predicted that an emblem of the firestone would be found in the Yucatan in the 1930s and portions of it brought to museums in Pennsylvania, Washington, and Chicago.[11] If the firestone could be preserved among the Central American descendants of the Atlanteans, perhaps it also survived in the Middle East, where Atlanteans migrated to Egypt after the final destruction of their homeland.

In fact, there are indeed several connections between the Urim and Thummim and Cayce's firestone. First, the *Jewish Encyclopedia* notes that, although most scholars have chosen to translate Urim as meaning simply "light," the word *urim* is actually derived from a word meaning "fire."

THE SAPPHIRE CONNECTION: URIM AND THUMMIM AND THE FIRESTONE

A second connection involves the gem sapphire that some biblical scholars believe could be the original stone used for the Urim and Thummin.[12] There are interesting references in which sapphire is described in Hebrew literature as a stone with unusual powers. For example, Hebrew mythology contains a story about the origin of Moses' staff, describing it as made of sapphire and engraved with the name of God. According to this story, the staff was carried by Adam out of the Garden of Eden as a gift from the Creator. It was then handed down through the biblical Patriarchs until, during the time of Joseph, it was taken by one of the high priests of Pharaoh. The priest stuck it into the ground where it became so firmly rooted no one could remove it or even touch it without being harmed. In some versions of the story, it had sprouted into a tree and those who tried to remove it were devoured. When Moses discovered it, he was able to remove it and to use its powers to, among other things, part the Red Sea.[13]

Later, in the Old Testament, we are told that the first set of tablets containing the Ten Commandments were broken after being dropped by Moses. (Exod. 32:19) He is then instructed by God to "Cut two stone tablets like the former . . . " in order that another set may be created. (Exod. 34:1) Rabbinical literature tells us that Moses used a block of sapphire from which to create the second set of tablets. The source goes even further to state that the sapphire "had been quarried from the solar disk."[14] Given that Moses was raised in Egypt, this is most likely a reference to the solar disk that symbolized the great god Amun–Re or Ra. In fact, the historian Josephus quotes the Gentile historian Apion's story that Moses was familiar with the sun worship practice of the Egyptians at Heliopolis. This practice was said to include prayers spoken while facing eastward in a building with an open–air roof.

Egyptian Winged Solar Disc—from Dover.

Nuiserre Sun Temple near Abu Sir, Egypt was once part of the sun worship tradition that centered at Heliopolis—photo by G. Little.

What is most intriguing, however, is that there appears to be a special link between sapphire and the firestone in the Cayce readings. A subscriber to the A.R.E. newsletter *Ancient Mysteries* noted that one of the Cayce readings tells of a Persian gem trader who carried with him " . . . pearls . . . the opal, the firestone, the lapis lazuli in Indo-China, yea the diamonds and rubies of some of the cities of gold."[15] He wondered if the firestone might be the name for a common gemstone that is conspicuously missing from the list—the sapphire. As he noted, at the microscopic level, the sapphire crystal is six-sided and that one form of it contains a brilliant, fire-like six- or twelve-pointed star. Also, a search of the Cayce readings on CD-ROM, strangely, reveals no references to the gem sapphire even though other commonly known gems of the ancient world are mentioned. Perhaps the readings used the term *firestone* to refer to sapphire and did so because they are one and the same.

Like Cayce's firestone, the sapphire can be used as a medium to create a laser. Interestingly, the impurity in the corundum (the mineral name for sapphire) that causes the star effect in the star sapphire is none other than rutile (titanium oxide). In our book, *The Lost Hall of Records*, we noted that rutile, when combined with a metal such as iron, can be used to create high frequency lasers. We further pointed out that raw hematite ore (iron oxide), such as that used by the Olmecs and the Maya to make sacred mirrors, often contains impurities of titanium. We concluded that these highly valued artifacts could be the "emblem" of the firestone that Cayce predicted would be found in the Yucatan. Since hematite is paramagnetic, the mirrors are also the best candidates for the magnetized stones that Cayce said were Atlantean artifacts used for spiritual communication.[16]

The connection between sapphire, rutile, and hematite is even more compelling, since the intense blue color of sapphire is produced only when atoms of both iron and titanium are present in the corundum. And, as if there weren't enough associations, the star formation is created because the rutile crystals form on the six-sided hematite crystals present in the corundum.[17]

WHERE ARE THE URIM AND THUMMIM NOW?

So, what happened to the Hebrew Urim and Thummim? No mention

**Statue from Olmec
site (La Venta, Mexico
ca. 1500 B.C.) of woman
in meditative pose with
polished   hematite
pendant fastened to
her chest—from BAE:
Bulletin, 153, 1952.**

can be found of them after the time of the Babylonian captivity (about
700–600 B.C.). Biblical scholars believe that the subsequent rise in prophetic revelation replaced the need for a specific oracle tool. Consequently, no such use is mentioned in the New Testament. It is believed
that, when the gift of the Holy Spirit was made available to everyone
after the resurrection and ascension of the Christ, a tool of this type
became unnecessary.[18] In other words, we do not need a special device
to have a direct relationship with the Creative Forces. As Cayce tells us,
we are all capable of manifesting psychic ability, since it is a soul quality. Through spiritual attunement and the practice of meditation, dream
guidance, and development of our natural intuition, we too can become high priests conversing one-on-one with the Divine.

   "Hence *intuitive* force is the better, for in this there may come more the union of the spirit of truth with Creative Energy; thus the answer may be *shown* thee, whether in Urim, in Thummim, in dream, in numbers, in *whatever* manner or form. For He *is* the strength of them all, and beareth witness *in* thee and through thee— if ye but do His biddings."[19]

20

The Parting of the Red Sea: Were Remains of Pharaoh's Army Found?

> . . . for as the Children of Promise passed through the Red Sea and were all baptized unto Moses, in the Cloud and in the Sea, the lesson then is as of the cleansing of the physical forces to that pure water, that, as is given, to be the work of spiritual forces . . .
>
> 900-132

The Cayce readings make it clear that the "Children of Promise" crossed the Red Sea during the Exodus, but the readings are curiously silent on the location and other details. This appears to have been due to a simple factor that occurred again and again during the readings: No one ever asked the sleeping Cayce to provide additional details. There have been many efforts to find artifacts and remains that could prove the story of Exodus, but the majority of archaeologists have long given up the hunt. However, there have been a few researchers who claim to have found the remains of Pharaoh's army that drowned in their pursuit of Moses. One of the most ardent of these was Ron Wyatt (now deceased).

Depending on who is asked, Wyatt was either one of the most pro-lific biblical archaeologists who ever lived or the most prolific hoaxer. In 1978, Wyatt claimed that he had a vision, showing him the location of the Red Sea crossing. Most archaeologists had looked in the shallow ends of the Red Sea, but Wyatt's vision told him that the crossing had occurred closer to the middle of the Red Sea, in what was considered to be impossibly deep water. The location of the site, the Gulf of Aqaba, is nearly 5,000 feet deep, but Wyatt found a 300-foot-deep ridge spanning the sea at that very spot. The ridge, essentially a high mount covered with sand, has since been verified by other researchers.

Wyatt and his divers reportedly found chariot wheels, human and horse bones, and other artifacts on the ridge. One of the wheels was covered in gold leaf. Members of the team then found a large, under-water stone pillar on the western side of the site. A similar pillar was found standing on the eastern side of the sea. The pillars were covered with inscriptions, which stated that they were erected to commemorate the site of the Red Sea miracle. Wyatt reported that Egyptian archaeolo-gists had dated the chariot wheels to about 1400 B.C. However, almost all archaeologists are completely skeptical about Wyatt's claim and most biblical scholars have become doubtful about the dates of the Exodus. Since that time, a few others claim to have replicated Wyatt's finds. Details of the finds can be found in L. Moller's *The Exodus Case*, and in two videos: *Exodus Discovered* and *Surprising Discoveries 2*.[1,2]

DID THE EXODUS REALLY HAPPEN?

Some scholars argue that the Exodus simply didn't happen. The dates appear to be off, the number of Israelites is impossibly high, and the miracles are too incredible to be believed. But over the past few years, evidence from several different sources is slowly supporting the Exodus story as actual history. For example, Cambridge University physicist Colin J. Humphreys' book,[3] *The Miracles of Exodus*, asserts that the biblical account of Exodus actually happened. Based on archaeological finds and clues from texts, Humphreys believes that there were only 20,000 Israelites led by Moses from Egyptian captivity, rather than the two million people traditionally thought to be freed. He suggests that a mis-translation of Exodus has created the idea that the story couldn't be a true account because of the impossibly large number of Israelites.

In addition, Humphreys concludes that the biblical Mount Sinai is actually located in Saudi Arabia, not on Egypt's Sinai Peninsula. The main reason for this assertion is that the Bible relates that Mt. Sinai was said to shake and emit fire and smoke. Thus it must have been an active volcano. The site that best fits this description is Mount Bedr, in north-western Saudi Arabia. His explanation of Moses' experience with the "burning bush" is related to the activity of the volcano. According to Humphreys, a vent of flammable volcanic gas was the source of the phenomenon. He also explains the route of the Exodus and the miracu-lous parting of seas. According to his theory, Moses took the group on an active trade route directly from Sinai to the Gulf of Aqaba on the Red Sea. (This is the location where Ron Wyatt found the underwater re-mains of chariots.)

Humphreys believes that a "wind tide" occurred, allowing the Israel-ites to cross the Sea over the exposed mount. A "wind set down" imme-diately followed, allowing the seas to rush back in, drowning Pharaoh's army. While Humphreys asserts that all of the events of Exodus were caused by natural events, including the plagues inflicted on the Egyp-tians, he adds that the timing of the events can truly be interpreted as miraculous.

21

Mary: Immaculate Conception and Apparitions

(Q) Neither Mary nor Jesus, then, had a human father?
(A) Neither Mary nor Jesus had a human father. They were one *soul* so far as the earth is concerned; because [else] she would not be incarnated in flesh, you see.

5749-8

Q) Please give that information concerning immaculate conception that can be given for me.
(A) As the spirit was made manifest in the body purified by consecration of purpose in the lives manifested in the earth, so might the spirit—with the brooding of the body itself—bring to the organs of flesh a body through which the spirit may itself manifest in the earth.

2072-4

Neither is there much indicated in sacred or profane history as to the preparation of the mother for that channel through which immaculate conception might take place. And this, the immaculate conception, is a stumblingstone to many worldly-wise.   5749-15

"**I** am the Immaculate Conception," proclaimed the beautiful lady in white during her sixteenth appearance to the fourteen–year old peasant girl Bernadette Soubirous, near

169

Lourdes, France, in 1858. These words so startled and impressed a previously skeptical Church hierarchy that their judgment of Bernadette's ecstatic visions was suddenly turned from doubt to belief.

The Catholic Church had just issued its doctrine of the Immaculate Conception in 1854. This teaching declared that Mary, the Mother of Jesus, was herself immaculately conceived in her own mother's womb, just as Jesus had been in Mary's womb. The apparition's use of the term "Immaculate Conception" to identify herself was particularly powerful since the uneducated, rural adolescent to whom she spoke was, in all likelihood, completely unfamiliar with its true meaning. Nor was it likely that Bernadette would have been aware of the theological debates on this very subject that had taken place within the Church since at least the seventh century.[1]

Grotto at Lourdes where Bernadette Soubirous had her vision of Mary— photo by L. Little.

Opening to spring on cave floor in Grotto at spot where Bernadette dug into the ground—photo by L. Little.

Miraculous Cures from the Water at Lourdes

Bernadette's eighteen separate visionary experiences occurred within a shallow cave beside the River Gave, just outside the small village of Lourdes, located in the foothills of the Pyrenees Mountains. She dutifully reported each vision to the local priest, who insisted that she find out the name of the beautiful lady. Until her sixteenth appearance, the lady refrained from identifying herself and would simply instruct Bernadette "to pray to God for sinners." During her ninth appearance, she asked Bernadette to drink from the spring and to wash in it. Since there was no water in the cave, Bernadette dropped to her knees and dug into the cave floor. A few minutes later, water bubbled up. Soon miraculous cures began to be attributed to the water from the spring. In one instance, sight was restored to a local stonemason who had been accidentally blinded twenty years earlier.[2]

View of Grotto (from Basilica built on top of the Grotto cliff) and visiting pilgrims—photo by L. Little.

Almost 150 years later, over five million international pilgrims visit the Grotto at Lourdes annually. Visitors include many with serious physical illnesses and incurable conditions who seek to be healed by washing or bathing in the spring water. As the Protestant writer Ruth Cranston outlines in her book, *The Miracles of Lourdes*, a nondenominational medical commission was set up in 1883 to document and validate claims of cure.[3] Using strict criteria and requiring multiple examinations, detailed medical history documentation, and an annual follow-up, the commission has so far certified only sixty-four cures as miraculous.[4]

Jewish historian and Oxford professor Ruth Harris studied the Lourdes phenomena extensively from the viewpoint of social and cultural anthropology in her recent book, *Lourdes: Body and Spirit in the Secular Age*. She notes that the early miracles attributed to Lourdes posed a great challenge to the mid-nineteenth-century medical community. The evidence was too overwhelming to be ignored and yet did not fit into the new movement toward science and modernity. For example, since many of the recipients of cures were women, the scientific experts of the nineteenth century often simply dismissed both the original diseases and the cures as being the result of a frequently diagnosed female condition they called "hysteria." Harris includes a quote from one physician who pronounced this diagnosis after the patient experienced pain upon his palpation of her lower abdomen in the area of the ovaries.

In addition, the cures were occurring during a time when there was a major power struggle between the secular world and the Church. For this reason, Harris believes that the medical commission at Lourdes has probably been overly cautious in its rejection of many of the cures.[5] Some modern investigators, such as Dr. Donald J. West (*Eleven Lourdes Miracles*), remain skeptical and assert that, with diseases such as cancer and tuberculosis, the cures could have been the result of changes in the patient's emotional well-being.[6]

In the book *Miracles: A Parascientific Inquiry into Wondrous Phenomena*, noted parapsychologist D. Scott Rogo points out that, although only a small number of cures at Lourdes have been officially verified, the histories of these few are astonishing. In one case, previously atrophied optic nerve tissue was mysteriously regenerated.[7] In another case, a five-year-old quadriplegic suffering from infantile encephalopathy received a complete cure.[8] Still more amazing is the case of Pierre de Rudder in which three centimeters of bone, which had been surgically removed due to an accident five years earlier, was restored almost instantaneously. The gap in the bone, which was in the middle of the lower leg, was so crippling that it created a condition in which the calf of the leg could be made to bend in half. (See the accompanying photograph of the individual taken after the miraculous cure.)[9, 10]

1893 photo of Pierre de Rudder showing his leg after it had healed.

A LINK WITH CAYCE'S ATLANTEANS?

There is an interesting link between the apparition at Lourdes and Cayce's story of Atlantis, since the Pyrenees is one of the areas of Atlantean migration. Filled with Paleolithic-era caves, this part of France has yielded many beautiful examples of stone age art. One of the finest is a three-dimensional sculpture of a horse carved in mammoth ivory, uncovered in a cave (*Grotte des Espelugues*) near the Lourdes apparition grotto, dating between 30,000 B.C. and 15,000 B.C. The Basque peoples of France and Spain are possibly descendants of this enigmatic stone age culture. Ruth Harris notes that the residents of Lourdes, " . . . with their infinitely various costumes and languages, were deemed the 'Indians' of France and colourfully represented as the indigenous peoples of an unadulterated race."[11] Bernadette was of pure Basque ancestry and was a product of a culture that Harris describes as " . . . still potentially in touch with cosmic elements."[12]

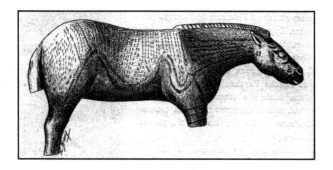

Drawing of three-dimensional sculpture of horse carved ca. 30,000-15,000 B.C. discovered in a cave near the apparition cave site—from M. Boule's *Les Hommes Fossiles* (1923).

Harris is especially impressed with the fact that Lourdes survived the dawning of the scientific age, and that it overcame many serious impediments to become the most popular Marian pilgrimage site of modern times. She emphasizes the importance of the support of the local villagers, particularly the women of both the upper and lower classes, as critical to its preservation and growth. Perhaps the spiritual attunement to the supernatural of Bernadette and her Basque neighbors, who were drawn to the sacred site and able to benefit from its healing powers, was particularly acute due to a genetic heritage from Atlantis.

Modern view of Fatima, Portugal, showing chapel and tree to the far right where apparition was seen—photo by L. Little.

Photo taken of apparition of Mary atop a Coptic Church as seen by several thousand people in Zeitoun, Egypt, in 1968—from *Page Research Library* (1975).

MARIAN APPARITIONS

So far, eleven apparitions of Mary have received official approval from the Roman Catholic Church. These include four in France (Rue de Bac—1830, LaSalette—1846, Lourdes—1858, and Pontmain—1871), two in Belgium (Beauraing—1932-1933 and Banneux—1933), and one each in Portugal (Fatima—1917), Japan (Akita—1973), Venezuela (Betania—1984), Mexico (Guadalupe—1531) and Ireland (Knock—1879). The Coptic Orthodox Church has recognized a Marian apparition near Cairo, Egypt (Zeitoun—1968). Several others, such as Garabandal in Spain (1961-1965) and Medjugorje in Yugoslavia (1981), have yet to receive official authentication from Church officials.[13]

The Cayce readings do not mention the Lourdes apparition or any of the other appearances of Mary around the world. Apparently, Cayce was never asked about them. However, the readings did discuss the process involved in immaculate conception and how it related to the very special Soul that incarnated as Mary and Jesus the Christ.

THE CAYCE READINGS ON MARY'S IMMACULATE CONCEPTION

There are at least six Cayce readings that discuss the concept of immaculate conception. One of these, given in 1937, states very clearly that Mary, like Jesus, did not have a human father.[14] However, a reading given in 1943 contains wording that could be viewed as contradictory:

> (Q) In Jewish history was anybody but Mary and Jesus immaculately conceived?
> (A) Mary was not immaculately conceived [according to Jewish history]. Jesus was. There have been others, but not in Jewish history.[15]

As can be seen, additional wording appears in brackets as an attempt to clarify the phrase in such a way that it would no longer be in opposition to the earlier reading. Cayce's stenographer, Gladys Davis, made a note to the file for this reading. It stated that plans had been made to do a follow-up reading in order to provide clarification, but that the reading was never obtained due to the overwhelming number of war-related reading requests.

Another 1937 reading seems to both contradict and confirm:

> (Q) Does the immaculate conception, as explained, concern the coming of Mary to Anne, or Jesus to Mary?
> (A) Of Jesus to Mary.
> (Q) Was Mary immaculately conceived?
> (A) Mary was immaculately conceived.[16]

One possible explanation for the contradictory statements is that there was something different about the conceptions of Jesus and Mary. This difference may in turn revolve around the fact that they were two halves of the same soul.

JESUS AND MARY: TWIN SOULS

(Q) Is the teaching of the Roman Catholic Church that Mary was without original sin from the moment of her conception in the womb of Ann, correct?

(A) It would be correct in *any* case. Correct more in this. For, as for the material teachings of that just referred to, you see: In the beginning Mary was the twin-soul of the Master in the entrance into the earth! [17]

According to the readings, all souls were androgynous in the beginning of human history, being both male and female. As discussed in an earlier chapter, the reincarnating Christ Soul, or Logos, first separated into male and female parts (Amilius and Lilith) in Atlantis sometime after 108,000 B.C.[18] Lilith reincarnated as Eve and later as Mary. This means that Jesus was incarnating into the womb of his twin soul, while Mary, by necessity, incarnated earlier into the womb of a soul that was not her twin.

WHAT IS "IMMACULATE CONCEPTION"?

Cayce described the process of immaculate conception as a spiritual form of reproduction that requires special preparation and a high level of attunement to the Creative Forces.

(Q) Explain anything that can be explained, by "physical reading," of immaculate conception.

(A) To be sure, this would have much more to do with the mental and spiritual aspects than the physical; though the body should be near to perfect coordination physically for such to be consummated in a body, and then the high mental and spiritual aspirations, desires and purposes. This information may be given much better from the spiritual and mental aspect—or approach.[19]

Then, the immaculate conception is the physical and mental so attuned to spirit as to be quickened by same.[20]

In other readings, Cayce indicates that all reproduction was completed in this way in the beginning of human history. The Logos or Christ Soul, for example, was able to manifest on the earth as Melchizedek without being born or dying in the physical sense.[21] However, this ability was lost over time as we gradually became entrapped in matter and lost the awareness of our connection to God.

HISTORICAL EVIDENCE FOR MARY'S IMMACULATE CONCEPTION

Although the Scriptures do not provide any information about the birth of Mary, apocryphal documents, such as the second-century *Protevangelium of James* and the *Gospel of Mary*, identify her parents as Anne and Joachim. Similar information is found in the Qur'an of Islam. These sources are further supported by the visions of the Catholic mystic Mary of Agreda (*The Mystical City of God*) whose writings, amazingly enough, were accepted by the infamous Spanish Inquisition of the seventeenth century. Interestingly, Mary of Agreda's confirmation of the Immaculate Conception of Mary was used to provide support for the Church's eventual declaration of that doctrine in 1854.[22]

In the recent A.R.E. Press book *Anna, Woman of Miracles*, by Carol Haenni and Vivian Van Vick, the story of Anne and Joachim and the Immaculate Conception of Mary is described in novel form, using information given in the Cayce readings, as well as details found in the visions of a German nun and mystic, Catherine Ann Emmerich. In this story, Anne and Joachim, a pious couple, are at first unable to conceive. At a time when Joachim has retreated to his sheep herd in the hills, an angel appears to each of them, telling them that they will indeed conceive and give birth to a very special child. They are instructed to meet at the "golden gate" near a temple in Jerusalem, and it is here that the Immaculate Conception occurs.

Biblical archaeology has identified Anne and Joachim's home and the golden gate in Jerusalem. They are believed to be located near the healing pool of water visited by Jesus and described in the Gospel of

John. (John 5:7) It is further theorized that this is the birthplace of Mary, since a Church of St. Mary is known to have existed there at least as early as A.D. 530. There is also a sheep gate nearby, which may represent the golden gate of the Immaculate Conception.[23]

FUTURE IMPLICATIONS

Cayce emphasized that immaculate conception is not only a natural, albeit latent, ability within each of us, but is "a natural law." In fact, he explained that it was this ability that allowed us to first project ourselves into matter.[24] He pointed out that Jesus and Mary's immaculate conceptions were a very important symbol that in fact marks a turning point in the evolution of humanity. We have entered a new period in which it is now possible for us to reclaim our true spiritual heritage and fully restore our connection to God.

> Then, that there has been an encasement was a beginning. Then there must be an end when this must be or may be broken; and this began at that particular period. Not the only—this particular period with Ann and then the Master *as* the son; but the *only* begotten of the Father in the flesh *as* a son *of* an immaculately conceived daughter! [25]

22

Wise Men from the East: The Rest of the Story

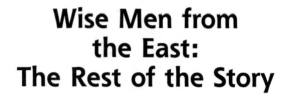

Hence we find the Wise Men as those that were seekers for the truth, for this happening; and in and through the application of those forces—as ye would term today psychic—we find them coming to the place "where the child was." Or they were drawn as those that were giving the thanks for this Gift, this expression of a soul seeking to show wayward man back to God.

5749-7

"We three Kings of Orient are, bearing gifts we traverse afar . . . "

So go the lyrics to the popular Christmas carol with which we are so familiar. It was written, of course, to commemorate the arrival of the Magi, or Wise Men, at the birth of the Christ Child. However, according to the Cayce readings, these visitors were not really kings, and there were more than three of them, arriving in several different groups from at least five different countries. In addition, although the modern Church celebrates their visitation on January 6, Cayce tells us that they were not actually presented to the Child until after the time of Mary's purification in accordance with Jewish Law (twenty-nine to forty days after birth).[1]

Cayce's expanded story comes together over multiple readings, including two in which individuals were told that they had been the Wise Men of the nativity story in previous lives. In Cayce's narrative, the true purpose and meaning of the gifts of gold, frankincense, and myrrh is explained, and we are even told why one group was routed by way of Herod rather than directly to the Christ Child. The readings also point out that the Wise Men's visit served to provide encouragement and support to Mary and those around her.

Wise Men guided by the Star of Bethehem—by Gustave Dore (1875).

WHAT THE BIBLE TELLS US

Despite the additional detail, amazingly the Cayce readings do not contradict the story we are told in the New Testament. One reason for this is that the Magi are mentioned briefly in only one of the books of the New Testament. (Matt. 2:1-16) Not only that, but the actual number of Wise Men is not even noted in that account. Bible scholars speculate that the tradition of the number *three* was taken from the number of gifts given (gold, frankincense, and myrrh). The Cayce readings indicate that there may have been as many as five different groups arriving before, during, and after the birth (although none were presented until the proper time).[2]

We are told in the Scriptures that the Magi had received a revelation of sorts and were following a star that they believed would lead them to the newly born "King of the Jews." For some reason they stopped in Jerusalem to inquire of the Child's whereabouts. Herod, the current head of the Jewish government under the Romans, felt immediately threatened and conspired with his chief scribes to use the Magi to locate this potential rival. The Magi, however, were directed in a dream not to return to Herod with the information. As a result, Herod ordered the death of all children in the area under the age of two years. Joseph, warned in a dream to flee with the Child to Egypt, escaped with the family.

WERE THE WISE MEN SPIRITUAL ADEPTS?

Although Bible scholars believe that the Wise Men came from Persia, Matthew's gospel does not specify the country of origin—just that they came from the East. Cayce states specifically that "They came from Persia, India, Egypt, and also from Chaldea, Gobi [China], and what is *now* the Indo or Tao land."[3] *Asimov's Guide to the New Testament* states that the Persian priests of the ancient Zoroastrian religion were called "magu," which in Latin becomes "magi."[4] This is particularly interesting in light of the Cayce readings that indicate that a previous incarnation of the Christ soul was Zend, the father of Zoroaster.[5]

The Jewish Encyclopedia tells us that the term *magi* was given to magicians from the Babylonian and Egyptian religions. The practice of magic was common throughout ancient Israel and the Middle East, especially among scholars. So-called white magic was differentiated from black magic (sorcery and worship of false gods) and was used primarily to counteract the latter form or for healing. "It was, however, only the practice of witchcraft that was prohibited, for a knowledge of magic was indispensable to a member of the chief council or of the judiciary . . . "[6]

It appears that white magic may have been a blanket term given to practices we would today list under psychic ability. In the Talmud, for example, Jesus is regarded as a magician. It is also noted that portions of these traditions, although condemned by some Hebrew factions, are said to be contained in the Kabala teachings.[7]

In the life readings for the former Wise Men, Cayce describes them as being both very spiritual and very intelligent and as having skills in astrology, astronomy, and mathematics.[8] They were spiritual seekers who were very much aware of the Hebrew Messianic prophecies. In one reading, Cayce refers to the Wise Men as " . . . those that subdued—not that were ruled by, but subdued the understandings of that in the earth—were considered, or were in the position of the wise, or the sages, or the ones that were holy; in body and mind, in accord with purposes." He further indicates that they found their way to the Christ Child " . . . in and through the application of those forces—as ye would term today psychic . . . "[9]

Magic Bowl with Hebrew Inscriptions found among the ruins of Babylon—from _The Jewish Encyclopedia_ (1905).

ESSENE RECORDS HIDDEN IN PYRAMID

Cayce also tells us that the Wise Men had spent time studying records of ancient wisdom kept in Egypt. It was from these records that they knew about the coming of the Messiah and the preparations made by a Jewish sect known as the Essenes.[10] An Essene teacher by the name of Judy was in charge of the records. She sent the first group of Wise Men to Herod in an attempt to undermine his relationship with the Romans and thus topple him from his throne. Her plan backfired and ultimately caused the death of many innocent children. As a result, she was told that, in this lifetime, she had to learn not to sit in judgment of others, regardless of their sins.[11]

Both Judy and another Essene teacher, Josie, were responsible for assisting in Jesus' education during his studies in Egypt, Persia, and India. In fact, a reading given in July of 1932 asserts that records of this training were in a pyramid "yet to be uncovered" and that the records might come to light between 1936 and 1940, "When there has been sufficient of the reckoning through which the world is passing in the present . . . " [13]

The readings also seem to indicate that these records contain the information studied by the Wise Men. Some have speculated that the thirteen papyrus books found in Nag Hammadi, Egypt, in 1945, and/or the Dead Sea Scrolls discovered shortly thereafter, could be the information to which Cayce was referring. Cayce also indicated that Herod's wife, who had contact with both the Essenes and the Wise Men, had written a history of this time period which was lost with the destruction of the Alexandria library.[13] In his recent book, *Edgar Cayce: An American Prophet*, Sidney Kirkpatrick states that portions of this narrative may still exist in the Vatican Library.[14]

THE MEANING OF THE GIFTS

In one reading regarding the training of the Christ Child by the Essenes, Cayce was asked, "What relation was there in the training with the three wise men?" His answer was that the presentation of the gifts of gold, frankincense, and myrrh by the Magi was a highly significant ritual, which prefigured the future development of Jesus and his initiation into his ministry later in life. "So they represent in the metaphysical sense the three phases of man's experience in materiality: gold, the material; frankincense, the ether or ethereal; myrrh, the healing force as brought with same; or body, mind, soul."[15]

Charles Fillmore notes in the *Metaphysical Dictionary* that the Wise Men are archetypal symbols which represent "the wisdom that is carried within the soul from previous incarnations. They are the inner realms of consciousness that, like books of life, have kept the records of past lives and held them in reserve for the great day when the soul would receive the supreme ego, Jesus."[17] In other words, they represent our higher self and our inner essence or individuality, as Cayce termed it. This inner wisdom serves to encourage and support our preparation for the birth of the Christ Consciousness into our limited consciousness.

WHAT HAPPENED TO THE WISE MEN?

The Cayce CD-ROM contains a magazine excerpt from 1967 recounting the Church tradition that the Wise Men were baptized by St. Thomas in India forty years after Bethlehem. They were subsequently ordained as Christian priests and eventually martyred for their faith. Their bodies were supposedly buried in the mosque of St. Sophia at Constantinople, later moved to a Cathedral in Milan, Italy, and then to Cologne, Germany. Their single elaborately ornamented, golden casket can today be viewed at the beautiful Cologne Cathedral. A first century tradition identifies the three Magi as Balthasar, Caspar, and Melchior. They were believed to be astrologers from Babylonia and Arabia and have been deemed the patron saints of travelers. [17]

23

Resurrection and Regeneration: Available to All?

... death hath no sting ... no power over those that know the Resurrection, [it] brought to the consciousness of man that power that God hath given to man, that may reconstruct, resuscitate, even every atom of a physically sick body ...   1158-5

Yet as He, the Father, hath given to each of you, "I have given my angels charge concerning thee, and they shall bear thee up, and thou shalt not know corruption."
                                                5749-6

In discussing the Resurrection of Christ, the Cayce readings present the incredible idea that the ability to regenerate and ultimately to resurrect the physical body is available to all of us. We can accomplish this through "a cleansing of the body, of the flesh, of the blood, in such measures that it may become illumined with power from on High" and by "surrendering all power ... unto the will of the Father."[1] John Van Auken's book *Edgar Cayce on Rejuvenation of the Body* gives a helpful synthesis of these readings and includes practical steps for maintaining spiritual, mental, and physical health. The ultimate goal, of course, is to be able to so spiritualize the material flesh that a new physical body is created, as Christ did at the Resurrection.

JUDEO-CHRISTIAN TRADITIONS FOR BODILY RESURRECTION

Cayce's ideas on physical regeneration, perhaps a conceptual stretch for many of us, are very much a part of Judeo-Christian tradition. According to the *Jewish Encyclopedia*, the Pharisees and the Essenes held the idea of bodily resurrection at some future Judgment Day as a critical tenet of their belief system. So much so, in fact, that they differentiated themselves from other Jewish groups of the time based on this single issue.[2]

Both the Nicene Creed and the Apostle's Creed, which are shared by most mainstream Christian denominations today, contain a declaration of belief in "the resurrection of the body," expected to occur at the end of the world. The apostles Paul and John discuss this specifically in the New Testament. (Rom. 8:11; 1 Cor. 6:14; John 5:24–25) In addition, the most recent version of the Roman Catholic Catechism states that "In death, the separation of the soul from the body, the human body decays and the soul goes to meet God, while awaiting its reunion with its glorified body. God, in His almighty power, will definitively grant incorruptible life to our bodies by re-uniting them with our souls . . . at the last day."[3]

REJUVENATION AND RESURRECTION IN ANCIENT TIMES

The Cayce readings indicate that regeneration was common to people in ancient times, but we devolved in spiritual consciousness, and it became necessary for the Christ to incarnate in order to raise our consciousness and thereby restore this ability. According to Cayce, the Egyptian priest Ra Ta and others of his time (ca. 10,000 B.C.) had life expectancies of "hundreds of years."[4] He describes Ra Ta as being able to "lay down the material weaknesses—and from those sources of regeneration *recreated* the body in its *elemental* forces."[5]

Among the Babylonians, there are legends of ancient patriarchs who lived thousands of years. The ages of their first five antediluvian kings range from the incredible totals of 43,200 years (Enmenluanna) to a "mere" 28,800 years (Alulim). Both Greek and Roman mythology con-

The seven tablets of Creation from Ancient Babylon—from D. MacKenzie's *Myths of Babylonia and Assyria* (1915).

tain stories of immortal beings who lived and interacted with mortal contemporaries in ancient times. The Book of Genesis lists the names of many pre-flood people who lived several hundred years, including Methuselah, who is said to have died at 969 years of age. In addition, Adam lived 930 years, Seth 912, Enoch 365, and Noah 950. All of these stories, although from different cultures, are similar in that life spans steadily decreased over time—as if this were an ability we have somehow lost.[6]

We are also told in the Old Testament that the bodies of both Enoch and Elijah were transferred to heaven at the end of their earthly lives. As outlined in Glenn Sanderfur's book, *Lives of the Master*, Cayce identifies Enoch as one of the previous incarnations of the Christ. The readings also note that another incarnation of Christ, Melchizedek, was "a living human being in flesh made manifest in the earth from the desire of the Father-God to prepare an escape for man" and was neither born nor died.[7] All three of these cases may be examples of a "glorified body" except that the individuals did not have to wait for the end times to be reunited with God. This idea is also found in Catholic doctrine, which states that the body and soul of Mary, the Mother of Jesus (and Jesus' twin soul, according to Cayce), was taken up to heaven at the end of her earthly life.[8]

Babylonian King Hammurabi receiving the Code of Laws from the Sun God—from D. MacKenzie's *Myths of Babylonia and Assyria* (♰915).

Preservation of the Body After Death

In her fascinating book *The Incorruptibles*, Joan Carroll Cruz explores the phenomenon of the preservation of the body after death as documented among various Christian saints. One of the most recent cases involved the famous visionary of Lourdes, Bernadette Soubirous of France, who died in 1879. (See earlier chapter on the miracles at Lourdes.) Cruz carefully differentiates between "the deliberately preserved" (mummified or embalmed remains), "the accidentally preserved" (via natural means such as the Bog Man of England), and "the incorruptibles," which are the focus of her book.

Beginning with St. Cecilia of Rome, who died in A.D. 177, and ending with Maria Pallotta, who died in 1905, Cruz describes over a hundred cases of highly spiritual persons whose bodies remained virtually undecomposed for decades or even centuries after death. In fact, in all cases, the body remained almost completely intact, was flexible, and was often sweetly scented. Many had been buried in moist environments that should have speeded their dissolution. In some cases, they were discovered to have been buried side by side with corpses that *had* experienced the expected amount of decay.

Another fairly recent case involved St. Charbel Makhlouf of Lebanon, who died on December 24, 1898. For forty-five days after his burial in Annaya, Lebanon, his tomb was observed to have been surrounded by an unnaturally bright light, prompting the monastery to request an exhumation. His preserved body, discovered floating in mud (he had been buried without a coffin), was removed from its flooded grave four months after burial. The body was re-exhumed several times during the twentieth century and examined by physicians who documented their findings. A final examination in 1950 showed no corruption, but by 1965 the body, which by that time was being kept in a sealed coffin, had finally decayed, leaving only reddish-colored bones.

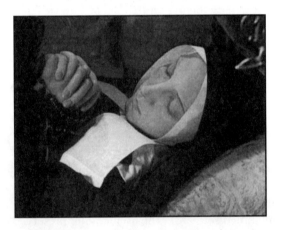

The incorrupt body of St. Bernadette Soubirous of Lourdes, France—photo 1909.

WHY WERE THESE BODIES PRESERVED?

Since the persons discussed in Cruz's book were all known to have led highly spiritual lives, are they examples of Cayce's regeneration of the body? If so, then why did the soul leave the body? And why did the body, in many cases, finally fall victim (sometimes centuries later) to decomposition? Also, why aren't the bodies of all spiritually evolved persons preserved? Cruz speculates that since many of these remains became the focus of miraculous healings, they may have served some higher purpose. She also shares that, when the dying St. Therese of the Little Flower was told that she would most likely be blessed by God with a preserved body after death, she remarked, "Oh, no, not that miracle." She did not receive it.[9]

Cayce tells us that, during Ra Ta's time, some of those who could have continued to rejuvenate instead "chose to lay aside the outer shell" when they had finished their earthly assignment.[10] For example, upon the completion of his life's purpose, Ra Ta "ascended into the mount and was borne away."[11] Interestingly, a woman who was told in a reading that she had been St. Cecilia (one of Cruz's incorruptibles) in a previous life was also told that she had been one of those who was of service in the Temple Beautiful during the time of Ra Ta.[12]

Since Cayce indicates that a part of the resurrection process is the ability to surrender to the will of God, perhaps Cruz's incorruptibles are at that point in the process. They have humbly shed their earthly bodies, which remain affected by the high vibrations of the souls who occupied them, and have left the timing of their bodily resurrection to the Will of the Creative Forces.

24

The Pentecost: Speaking with Tongues of Fire

In those activities then that followed the Crucifixion, and the days of the Pentecost, and the sermon or teachings—and when there was beheld by Lucius the outpouring of the Holy Spirit, when Peter spoke in tongues—or as he spoke in his *own* tongue, it, the message was *heard* by those of *every* nation in their *own* tongue . . .   294-192

One of the most mysterious and unaccountable stories of the New Testament appears in the second chapter of the Acts of the Apostles. At this point, Christ has just recently ascended from the Mount of Olives. The Apostles and almost 120 other followers are gathered together in prayer "with one accord in one place. And suddenly there came a sound from heaven as of a rushing mighty wind, and it filled all the house where they were sitting." Next they noticed that over the head of each person appeared "cloven tongues like as of fire . . . And they were filled with the Holy Ghost, and began to speak with other tongues as the Spirit gave them utterance." (Acts 2:2–4)

Peter and the other disciples then went into

the streets and preached to Jewish pilgrims "out of every nation" present in Jerusalem on that day. The people in the crowd were amazed that they could each hear these Galileans speaking to them in their native language. Peter's inspired discourse is recorded in detail and contains references to Hebrew scripture that explain the Apostles' sudden, unusual abilities and the significance of the life of Jesus of Nazareth. The Apostles were now able to perform "many wonders and signs." (Acts 2:44) We are told that as a result, 3,000 were converted that day, which is considered to mark the beginning of the Christian church.

The Apostles and Mary in the Upper Room during the Descent of the Holy Spirit at Pentecost—Gustave Dore (1875).

THE CAYCE READINGS ON THE PENTECOST

The Cayce readings provide some verification of the Pentecost story, since they indirectly indicate that a firsthand witness to these events wrote the Book of Acts. This witness was a man of Roman and Greek heritage named Lucius of Cyrene, who received a brief mention in the Bible as an associate and teacher of Paul. (Acts 13:1 and Rom. 16:21) Bible experts are uncertain as to the identity of the author of the Acts of the Apostles, but they do agree that someone who was not Jewish wrote it. According to a 1939 reading, Lucius was in fact one of Edgar Cayce's most prominent past lives. Interestingly, the readings stated that Cayce was not told of this particular past life until only a few years before his death in order to keep it from inflating his ego.[1]

Several other people were told in the readings that they had witnessed the events of the Pentecost in a past life. Some had been among those converted on that day.[2,3] When asked how those present at the Pentecost were able to hear the Apostles speaking in their native tongues, Cayce replied that it was "the activity of the spirit" within the *receiver* of the message.[4] Thus, the confusion of languages, which had been the result of the sin of mankind at the Tower of Babel, was temporarily removed through the power of the Holy Spirit.

THE CAYCE READINGS ON SPEAKING IN TONGUES

Some religions have interpreted the Apostles' experience at Pentecost as an ability to speak in tongues in a type of ecstatic prayer known as *glossolalia*. In fact, the New Testament does indicate that after the Pentecost some of the early Christians experienced this ability. For example, Paul lists several metaphysical gifts in his letter to the Corinthians, including the ability to "speak in tongues" as if they were quite common at that time. (1 Cor. 13:1–40) He then goes to great lengths to further explain how speaking in tongues should be utilized for spiritual growth and not for personal pride. The early church fathers indicate that this phenomenon continued to be commonly experienced for about two centuries.[5] It has resurfaced in the twentieth century through the new Pentecostal and charismatic movements within many different Christian denominations.

Although Cayce indicates that the Apostles' experience at Pentecost was the result of the spiritual experience of the listener, he refers to the other type of speaking in tongues as well. "To some there is given the interpretation of tongues, or the interpretation of words or signs or symbols. This is what is meant by interpreters of tongues in the Holy Writ."[6]

He described how this works in more detail in a past-life reading given for a woman who had been among the Essene maidens on the temple steps when Mary was chosen to be the mother of Jesus: "The entity was among those who saw that vision on the stairs, when the first choice of the maidens was made. The entity knew then of the voice of the unseen forces as were aroused within the groups, that made for the speaking with the unusual tongues; not unknown yet unusual tongues, or the ability to make known their wishes to many in many tongues."[7] Thus, it seems that the readings are telling us that the Presence of the Holy Spirit created not only the ability to understand other languages, but also a secondary ability to speak in "unusual tongues."

However, echoing Paul in Corinthians, the readings warn that this type of prayer, although meaningful, is not an end in itself. "For, phenomena—or phenomenon—is but an awakening to that in which there *are* to be choices of activity upon the part of the self, and is as an assurance and not to be boasted of, nor to be other than that of the *answering* to that within. For, thy body—as ye experienced then—is indeed the temple of the living God, and there He hath promised to meet thee. There His awareness—even as then—may be seen, may be heard, may be felt, may be tasted—yea, experienced in all manners; but the reality is to self, not to others."[8]

HISTORICAL EVIDENCE FOR THE GATHERING OF PENTECOST

There is historical support for the presence of a large number of visitors in Jerusalem from multiple nations, since the Christian Pentecost event is known to have occurred during an important Hebrew harvest festival. Pentecost means "fiftieth day" and was celebrated by the Jews on the fiftieth day after Passover. It is based on the ancient Canaanite tradition of presenting the first fruits of the harvest to God. Pilgrims journeyed great distances to a central sacred location to make their offerings and to receive a blessing from Yahweh. It is believed that some of the nations listed in the Book of Acts represent locations where the Lost Tribes of Israel were scattered during the Babylonian Captivity period of the sixth century B.C. [10]

In biblical numerology, the number "50" is significant in that it contains seven 7s plus 1 and represents fulfillment. Bible scholars note that, while the Passover is a celebration using unleavened bread (a sacrifice, as at the Crucifixion), the Jewish tradition for the Pentecost included the addition of yeast to bread that was then offered to Yahweh. For these early Christians, this symbolism was reflected in the "addition" or infusion of the Holy Spirit on the Pentecost and was the fulfillment of the promise made by Christ at the Ascension.[11]

Drawing of topographical features of Jerusalem showing location of Mount Zion (Sion) left of center—from The Jewish Encyclopedia (1905).

The Tower of David near his tomb on Mount Sion as it appears in modern times—from The Jewish Encyclopedia (1905).

The Citadel of Mount Zion (Sion)—from The Jewish Encyclopedia (1905).

CAN THE SITE OF PENTECOST BE CONFIRMED?

There is little that researchers could do to verify such a supernatural story. However, surprisingly, there are a large number of historical accounts that identify a building on Mount Sion (or Zion) as the actual location of the Christian Pentecost event. The first of these accounts goes back to the time of the Roman Emperor Hadrian, who visited Jerusalem in A.D. 130. Over the years, various church buildings were erected on the site. The present structure, called the Cenacle, was rebuilt and placed under the protection of Franciscan monks, beginning in the thirteenth century. Visitors can tour the Gothic–style chapel, which is also said to be the location of the Last Supper as well as the place where Mary, the mother of Jesus, "lay down to sleep" at the time of her death. The Russian abbot Daniel (A.D. 1106) wrote that it was the home of St. John the Evangelist.

Eusebius, Bishop of Caesarea during the time of Constantine, states that the Christian church spread from Mount Sion throughout the world and that the upper room of the original building was the place where the resurrected Christ visited the Apostles before the Ascension. It is also believed to have been the location of the Jerusalem church headed by St. James.

Interestingly, Mount Sion is the highest point in Jerusalem, and the Mount of Olives is the second highest. This provides a link to ancient cultures throughout the world, since many of the most sacred sites are built on high places. The legendary tomb of the Old Testament's David is believed to be nearby on Mount Sion. This gives support to the identification of the upper room, since Peter refers to David's tomb as being nearby in his Spirit–inspired speech on the day of Pentecost. Scholars, however, debate whether Peter's reference was based on fact or simply according to the beliefs of the day. Today the Tomb of David is a Jewish sanctuary, although it has been under the control of both Christians and Moslems at various times throughout history. The Pentecost building on Mount Sion suffered a similar fate and was even claimed by the Crusaders at one point.[12]

CREATING YOUR OWN PENTECOST

As Anne Read points out in her book, *Edgar Cayce on Jesus and His Church*, the readings emphasize that the people present in the upper room on Mount Sion were in a heightened state of readiness and attunement. They expected to experience something special that the readings say is available to all of us here and now. We have only to seek.[13]

(Q) What is the Holy Church?
(A) That which makes for the awareness in the heart of the individual . . . For here ye may find the answer again to many of those questions sought concerning the Spirit, the Church, the Holy Force that manifests by the attuning of the individual; though it may be for a moment."[14]

25

El Camino de Santiago: Shrine of St. James or Atlantean Link?

As each of the twelve Apostles represented major centers or regions or realms through which consciousness became aware in the body of the earth itself, so did He find—as in thine own self ye find—those twelve stumblingstones . . . These are the price of flesh, of material consciousness, and are only passing. 2823-1

For over a thousand years, spiritual pilgrims from all over Europe have walked the sacred "Camino de Santiago" (Way of St. James). Once part of a Roman trade route with several starting points, all trails lead to the Cathedral of Santiago near where the westernmost tip of Spain juts out into the Atlantic. The journey is taken for the purpose of spiritual renewal, repentance, and to ask for special favors from the Apostle James, whose bones are said to be buried at the Cathedral. The most popular routes consist mainly of primitive footpaths that run through the Pyrenees Mountains. Since many travelers are on foot or bicycle, the journey is challenging and usually takes several months.[1] Shirley MacLaine was one of those drawn to walk the Camino and described her unusual experiences in a book.[2]

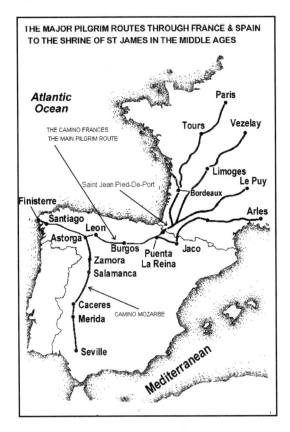

THE MAJOR PILGRIM ROUTES THROUGH FRANCE & SPAIN TO THE SHRINE OF ST JAMES IN THE MIDDLE AGES

Atlantic Ocean

Paris

Tours

Vezelay

THE CAMINO FRANCES
THE MAIN PILGRIM ROUTE

Limoges
Le Puy

Saint Jean Pied-De-Port

Bordeaux

Finisterre

Arles

Santiago
Leon

Astorga

Burgos
Zamora
Salamanca

Puenta
La Reina

Jaco

Caceres
Merida

CAMINO MOZARBE

Seville

Mediterranean

Map of France and Spain showing various routes of the Camino de Santiago—by G. Little.

HOW DID THE BODY OF ST. JAMES END UP IN SPAIN?

According to Spanish legend, one of the two Apostles named James lived and preached in Spain for several years after the Pentecost, eventually returning to Jerusalem, where he was martyred. His disciples, with angelic assistance, secretly transported his body by boat back to his beloved Spain. After landing on the Atlantic coast of northwestern Spain, they carried his body a short distance via ox-cart and buried it in the exact spot where the oxen mysteriously stopped. The Way of St. James is also referred to as *Camino de Compostela*, the last word meaning, "field of star" because of the nature of its later rediscovery during the ninth century. A hermit named Pelagius had a vision in which he saw a bright star, surrounded by a ring of smaller stars, shining over a deserted area in the hills. He reported it to the local bishop who, upon investigation, uncovered a tomb at the site containing three bodies. The bishop, by some unknown rationale, determined that the remains belonged to the Apostle James and two companions. King Alfonso II (A.D. 791–824) confirmed the discovery and immediately declared James to be the patron saint of Spain. A monastery and chapel were originally built over the site where the Cathedral of Santiago stands today.[3]

THE CONTROVERSY CONCERNING THE TWO APOSTLES

Despite the popularity of the pilgrimage over so many centuries, the Roman Catholic Church and biblical scholars can find no evidence that either of the two Apostles named James visited Spain, much less that one of them was buried there. Also, there is a structure in Jerusalem known as the Tomb of James, dating ca. A.D. 44, which was supposedly erected on the site where one of the Jameses was martyred. Although the Bible provides only sketchy information about the activities of the twelve Apostles, the Tomb of James does correlate with the book of Acts, which reports that Herod murdered "James, the brother of John," around that time. (Acts 12:1–2) However, according to several books of the New Testament, another James later emerges. Called "the brother of Jesus," he was the leader of the Church in Jerusalem and the author of the Epistle of James. (Gal. 1:19)

The Cayce readings contain several references to both of the Jameses and seem overall to indicate that they were two different people. There is one slightly confusing reading in which Cayce appears to identify James, "the brother of the Lord," as both the one martyred by Herod and the one who later headed the Church.[4] However, Cayce is very specific in asserting that Mary and Joseph conceived three additional children by conventional means, beginning some ten years after the birth of Jesus. The oldest of these, he said, was the Apostle James who headed the Church.[5] There is no mention in the readings of either James being associated with Spain.

Robert Eisenman provides an exhaustive review of the controversy of the two Jameses in his recent book, *James, the Brother of Jesus*. Utilizing his many years of study of the Dead Sea Scrolls and other historical documents, he concludes that most likely there was only one James, one of several actual brothers of Jesus, and that his role as a major authority figure in the early Church was deliberately obscured and minimized by Church historians. This James was both very holy and very militant, perhaps even participating in the Jewish revolt against the Romans in A.D. 70. One Cayce reading appears to support this by indicating that James' death was brought about as a result of a riot that he caused. As Cayce commented, "not incorrectly were James and John called the sons of thunder."[6]

JAMES, THE SON OF THUNDER

Eisenman's theory fits well with Spanish legends, since many of the metaphysical phenomena associated with St. James have a military connection. Apparitions of St. James have been witnessed frequently in both Spain and Central America. For example, during the Spanish Christian and Moslem War of A.D. 844, he was seen leading the Spanish army in battle, mounted on a white horse. He was also said to have made a similar appearance with Cortez during the latter's conquest of Mexico in the sixteenth century.[7]

In the book *Maya Cosmos*, Maya expert Linda Schele describes how the Quiche Maya utilized the power and patronage of the Spanish "god" Santiago to help them successfully defeat the Salvadorans during a 1906 battle. Their Maya name for him means "Venus Morningstar," since the ancient Maya venerated Venus as a symbol of war and death. The modern Chorti Maya have incorporated Christian traditions into their native spirituality by equating Santiago with the god of storms, "who sends the thunder and commands the rains" as well as, oddly enough, the Milky Way.[8]

Clam shell symbol for St. James carved on buildings in Salamanca, Spain to mark the Camino—photo by L. Little.

City of Burgos, Spain—photo by L. Little.

COULD THE WAY OF ST. JAMES HAVE AN EVEN EARLIER HISTORY?

It is known that many of the trails of the Camino were actually in existence well before the time of Christ, as Roman trade routes, and possibly even earlier, when this part of Europe was populated by the

Celts. Many of the buildings along the route are decorated with a floral design that some believe resembles Celtic sun worship images.[9] However, it is likely that they originated even earlier, since megalithic tombs and cave art dating back as far as 30,000 B.C. have been found throughout the area.

In 2002, paleontologists uncovered an axe head among a pit of bones at a 350,000-year-old burial site, which may be proof that early hominids were capable of "intentional or symbolic thought." The hand-sized, triangular rock made of quartz appeared to have been deliberately placed within the burial. Researchers also believe that the bodies were placed in the cave one by one in order that they might be buried together as if they belonged to a special group. The discovery was made at a site called Pit of Bones, located in a cave at Atapuerca in Central Spain near the city of Burgos. That city is one of the traditional stopping points along the Camino.[10]

Even more compelling is the fact that the Pyrenees Mountains are occupied by the mysterious Basque culture, which archaeologists believe moved into the region between 13,000 B.C. and 8,000 B.C. According to the Cayce readings, the Pyrenees, as well as parts of France and Spain, were one of the places to which residents of Atlantis migrated prior to the 10,500 B.C. destruction of their islands in the Atlantic.[11] This is especially interesting, since all of the ancient trails of the Camino eventually converge and lead to the coastal town of Cape Finisterre on the westernmost point of Spain. In fact, for some unknown reason, medieval pilgrims frequently traveled on from Santiago to the Chapel of Nuestra Senora (Our Lady) at Finisterre as if following some more ancient tradition.[12]

AN ATLANTEAN CONNECTION?

The name Finisterre itself is derived from two Latin words meaning "the end or edge of the earth." During Roman times, the Camino routes were nicknamed *la voje ladee*, "the Milky Way." It is thought that this was because that pattern of stars appeared to point toward the west, where the sun disappeared into the ocean.[13] However, ancient creation myths, the Milky Way, and even St. James are strangely linked among the native cultures of Central America.

The ancient Maya, who the Cayce readings say are descended from another group of migrating Atlanteans, believed that the seasonal movement of the Milky Way across the night sky retold the story of the Creation.[14] In the Maya's Creation story, an Atlantean-type character called Itzamna, or First Father, paddled across the ocean from the east so that he could be "reborn and create a new universe." Modern Chorti Maya in Honduras hold a ceremony on the Spanish Feast of Santiago (July 25) that focuses on the Milky Way, which they call "the road to Santiago." On that day, as Schele points out, the Milky Way runs perpendicular to the ecliptic (the movement of the sun from east to west), forming what the ancient Maya depicted as the Foliated Cross, or the Tree of Creation.[15]

Could it be that the Camino de Santiago of Spain is the modern remnant of the route taken by Atlanteans migrating to a "New World"? If so, then perhaps the longevity of its sacred and spiritual significance derives from this earlier seminal event. Its current association with a highly revered Christian saint, who most likely never set foot there, may only be a relatively modern translation.

26

Paradise:
Where and When?

For heaven is that place, that awareness where the
Soul—with all its attributes, its Mind, its Body—be-
comes aware of being in the presence of the Creative
Forces, or one with same. That is heaven.   262-88

We humans, in our many cultures and
religions from the East to the West, have always told tales of a special place called Paradise. The word *pairidaeza* has its origins in the
Avestan language of Zoroastrian teachings,
meaning a special "enclosure." In Greek,
paradeisos means a select "park." Many equate
these words with the original "park," the Garden of Eden, that special place where God
walked and talked with us. On the cross, in his
final moments, Jesus referred to this place
when he told the thief who was dying next to
him, "This day you will be with me in Paradise." (Luke 23:43)

Paradise—the word means so much to us. It
is a place of supreme happiness, extreme
beauty, and endless peace and safety. It is
where the righteous live after life on earth.
However, in strict Christian teachings, it is an
intermediate place for the departed souls of the
righteous awaiting the final resurrection of the
dead unto eternal life with God and Christ.

Paradise – Gustave Dore (1875)

Cayce's readings support this *interim* view of Paradise. When he was asked what Jesus meant by his statement to the thief on the cross, Cayce answered: "The inter-between; the awareness of being in that state of transition between the material and the spiritual phases of consciousness of the Soul."[1]

Near–death experiences (NDE) have added to our understanding of paradise. Most who have had a NDE return to this world more loving, peaceful, and unafraid of death. Their experience in the inter–between affected them profoundly, mostly in their outlook and attitude toward life.

Buddhists have a concept that also seems to separate the ultimate heavenly reality with an interim paradise. According to some of their key teachings, *nirvana*—ultimate bliss—is of such a nature as to render the experiencer useless in this world. It is a heavenly state so far from earthly reality that there is no connection between the two. However, *bodhisattva* consciousness, literally meaning "enlightened existence," is an interim state of consciousness of an advanced spiritual being who has chosen not to pass into full *nirvana*, but to continue in the round of rebirths in order to help others. *Bodhisattva* consciousness is an inter-between state in which the soul is enlightened, but remains an active helper in the borderlands around the physical world and in the world. Cayce seems to have supported this view of Paradise consciousness when he answered a request to suggest a doctor who could carry out the treatments by saying, "There are those in Paradise who may work with these suggestions . . . "[2] Doctors from Paradise?

Kingdom of Heaven—Kingdom of God

Cayce identifies a difference between the Kingdom of God and the Kingdom of Heaven. The Kingdom of Heaven is within us, and Jesus likened it to many things: to seed that a man sowed in his field; to leaven a woman hid in three measures of meal; to a treasure hidden in a field; to a pearl of great price; and to a net cast into the sea (Matt. 13). Jesus said that one who has been made a disciple of the Kingdom of Heaven was like "a householder who brings forth out of his treasure things new and old." (Matt. 13:52) The Kingdom of Heaven is attained through "the consciousness, the awareness of the activity of the spirit of truth in and through us, as individuals," says Cayce, individuals in the finite realms of life. He explains that "the individual does not *go* to heaven, or paradise, or the universal consciousness, but it *grows* to same; through the use of self in those things that are virtues . . . "[3] Living in virtue and giving aid to others brings that happiness that is associated with the Kingdom of Heaven. It is a growing thing, like an unseen seed planted in good soil or unseen leaven kneaded into bread dough.

On the other hand, the Kingdom of God is a conscious state of One-ness with the Infinite. It may be experienced while one is still walking the path, helping others in daily life, and growing to full heavenly con-sciousness. The Kingdom of God may be spontaneously experienced—a flash of illumination, a moment in the Presence, an overwhelming real-ization of complete at-onement with God. The Kingdom of God has never changed and does not develop. We live in it; whether we're aware of it or not. As Cayce says, "One is the experiences of the *finite* [Kingdom of Heaven]; the other is the glory with the Oneness in the *infinite* [Kingdom of God]."[4] This may explain how Jesus could say that "heaven and earth will pass away," but his words, his essence will never pass away. (Matt. 24:35)

Like *bodhisattvas*, we may all attain heavenly consciousness and live with it for a very long time. But eventually, all merge with the infinite, eternal Source. In that ultimate bliss, *nirvana*, oneness, all animated material projections are devolved.

There is an implication in the Cayce work that as long as we are incarnate—in the body—we cannot *fully* realize or maintain a consciousness completely connected with the Kingdom of God. It's somewhat akin to the Buddhist idea of *nirvana* being so alien to this world as to be impossible to sustain while actively functioning here. In one of his readings, Cayce said the spiritual entity and superconsciousness are a "thing apart from anything earthy," and can only be experienced by lifting oneself up into them. He explains that "the earthly or material consciousness is ever tempered with material conditions; the superconsciousness with the consciousness between soul and spirit, and partakes of the spiritual forces principally." He says that "we find only projections of subconscious and superconscious . . . in dreams, visions," unless we lift ourselves "into the superconscious forces," which are the higher spiritual forces. Nevertheless, there is a connection between our earthly selves and our godly selves because the superconscious is affected by and helps affect our spiritual discernment and development, which occurs while we are in the earth realms and physical life.[5]

HEAVEN ON EARTH?

We may know "heaven on earth or in the earth, or in flesh." It is the "destiny of those that are willing, who have had their minds, their bodies, their souls cleansed in the blood of the Lamb. How? By being as He, a living example of that He, the Christ, professed to be . . . "[6] "'Flesh and blood hath not revealed this unto thee, but my Father which is in heaven.' Heaven? Where? Within the hearts, the minds; the place where Truth is made manifest!"[7]

In the Revelation, a new heaven and a new earth are spoken of. Cayce says that "as the desires, the purposes, the aims are to bring about the whole change physically, so does it create in the experience of each soul a new vision, a new comprehension." He asks, "Is this not a new heaven, a new earth?"[8]

HEAVEN: A PLACE OR A STATE OF MIND?

Some wonder if heaven is just a state of consciousness or an actual place. Some point to Jesus' comments to Mary in the garden after His resurrection, "Touch me not, for I have not ascended to my Father." (John 20:17) Cayce says this would indicate to some " . . . that the heaven and the Father are somewhere else—a place of abode, the center about which all universal forces, all energies must turn . . . For heaven is that place, that awareness where the Soul—with all its attributes, its Mind, its Body—becomes aware of being in the presence of the Creative Forces, or one with same. That is heaven."[9]

As Cayce often taught, the Second Coming begins within our hearts and minds, in that awareness where our souls are one with the Creative Forces, or God, our unseen Creator. Where has Jesus been for two thousand years? In that unseen oneness. From where is he returning? From out of that unseen, universal oneness into the seen, individualness of incarnate life. We don't have to wait. We can go into the oneness anytime. It is an awareness that our soul can know. The kingdom of God is within us. If we seek, we will find it. That's a promise.

27

The Mystery of the Second Coming

For He will one day come again, and thou shalt see Him as He is, even as thou hast seen in thy early sojourns the glory of the day of the triumphal entry and the day of the Crucifixion, and as ye also heard the angels proclaim "As ye have seen Him go, so will ye see Him come again." Thou wilt be among those in the earth when He comes again. Glory in that, but let it be rather the one reason why ye keep the faith, the faith in the coming of the Lord, to call those who have been faithful; that they, as He prayed, "may be where I am, and may behold the glory which I had with thee before the worlds were."   3615-1

For nearly four hundred years prior to the First Coming, nothing happened in Israel of any spiritual significance, or so we are led to believe. Does this mean that the Light came out of the darkness of those times? Or was there a small, dedicated group going about the preparation for the coming of the Messiah, cleansing their minds, hearts, and bodies? According to Edgar Cayce's vision on the subject, the Essenes were quietly preparing the way for the promised Messiah.

Now, today, we find ourselves once again waiting and wondering about the Second Coming. Is it to happen in our lifetimes? Is it

The New Jerusalem—Gustave Dore (1875).

possible to know when it is going happen? After all, the prophecy states
that even the Son does not know when the Father will send Him again.

For many of us, Cayce's readings indicate that many major spiritual
events will occur in our lifetimes. Yet, as we begin this new millennium,
it becomes unclear as to whether we misinterpreted his readings or
they were simply off the mark. Didn't reading 5748-5 say that the Messiah would return in 1998? Didn't reading 5749-5 say that Edgar Cayce
was the "forerunner of that influence in the earth known as the Christ
Consciousness, the coming of that force or power into the earth that has
been spoken of through the ages?"

This particular reading was given to a small group who were told by
Cayce that each of them, in various incarnations, had written and taught
that the Second Coming would be soon: " . . . in your ignorance and in
your zeal" you have talked and written about this "that would influence

the activities in the religious or spiritual life of individuals through the ages . . . " Yet, he goes on to say that they had not fully understood the meaning of the promise of a Second Coming, or even the meaning of the First Coming! According to Cayce, the First Coming was not intended to create a perfect life on earth, as Judas believed and attempted to force, but rather to make earth life a means to correcting spiritual life! "He, our Lord and our Master, was the first among those that put on immortality that there might be the opportunity for those forces that had erred in spiritual things" to know through their material development, their earth life, the difference between "spirit that was good and spirit that was in error," and choose good while subduing error. "He has come in all ages when it has been necessary for the understanding to be centered in a *new* application of the same thought, 'God *is* Spirit and seeks such to worship him in spirit and in truth!'"[2]

The disciples actually believed the Second Coming would occur in their own lifetimes. Most Christians over the past 2,000 years have longed for it to happen in their lifetimes. And here we are again, at the turn of the millennium, looking for the Second Coming. In one reading, Cayce says, " . . . the merciful kindness of the Father has, in the eyes of many, delayed the Coming, and many have cried even as the parable He gave, 'We know not what has become of this man. Show us other gods that may lead us in this day . . . ' Yet, as He has given, in patience, in listening, in being still, may ye know that the Lord doeth all things well. Be not weary that He apparently prolongs His time . . . "[3]

THE SECOND COMING BEGINS WITHIN US

Cayce explains that the Second Coming *begins* within the heart and mind of each of us. We must obliterate the spirit of error while strengthening the spirit of good, which can then radiate out to others. This is the influence "that will save, regenerate, resuscitate, *hold*—if you please—the earth in its continued activity toward the proper understanding and proper relationships . . . to that which is in Him alone." If this work is being done by us, as the Essenes did theirs, then, Cayce says, "He may come in body to claim His own."[4]

But Cayce exclaims that He is already here, working hard and in need of our help: "Is He abroad today in the earth? Yea, in those that cry unto Him from every corner; for He, the Father, hath not suffered His soul to see corruption; neither hath it taken hold on those things that make the soul afraid. For, He *is* the Son of Light, of God, and is holy before Him. And He comes again in the hearts and souls and minds of those that seek to know His ways."

Cayce concludes this reading with this promise, "Ye, too, may minister in those days when He will come in the flesh, in the earth, to call His own by name."[5]

When Cayce was pressed on when the Second Coming will happen, he said: "When those that are His have made the way clear, *passable*, for Him to come."[6] The spirit of "hate, prejudice, selfishness, backbiting, unkindness, anger, passion, and those things of the mire that are created in the activities of the sons of men" must be subdued and obliterated.[7] This is the preparation work before us.

Let's be up and about this work, then. Let's eliminate the spirit of error and accentuate the spirit of good within ourselves and radiate it out to others. Not necessarily in grand ways, but a cup of water given in His name, a smile in His name, a visit in His name, a kind word, and so on. (Matt. 25:34–40) These little things penetrate the darkness with light, with love, and open the way for Him to return. " . . . then do with a might that your hands find to do to make for the greater manifestations of the love of the Father in the earth."[8] Let's take this to heart and do with our might what we can to help. Then, when He comes, He'll find us with oil in our lamps and lights in our hearts and minds.

28

Earth Changes, Quantum Physics, and the Science of Prophecy

As to the changes physical again: The earth will be broken up in the western portion of America. The greater portion of Japan must go into the sea. The upper portion of Europe will be changed as in the twinkling of an eye. Land will appear off the east coast of America. There will be the upheavals in the Arctic and in the Antarctic that will make for the eruption of volcanos in the Torrid areas, and there will be shifting then of the poles—so that where there has been those of a frigid or the semi-tropical will become the more tropical, and moss and fern will grow.   3976-15

(Q) Are the physical changes in Alabama predicted for 1936-38 to be gradual or sudden changes?
(A) Gradual.
(Q) What form will they take?
(A) To be sure, that may depend upon much that deals with the metaphysical, as well as to that people called actual or in truth! for, as understood—or should be by the entity—there are those conditions that in the activity of individuals, in line of thought and endeavor, keep oft many a city and many a land intact through their application of the spiritual laws in their associations with individuals. This will take more of the form here in the change, as we find, through the sinking of portions with the following up of the inundations by this overflow.   311-10

215

Many of us who have studied the Cayce readings have puzzled over the apparent contradictions among the earth changes predictions. Some of the readings indicate a very sudden and cataclysmic change beginning in 1998, while others state that the effect will be of a gradual nature. The 1994 A.R.E. *Earth Changes Circulating File* with an introduction by Kevin Todeschi provides a listing of all of the earth changes readings, both those describing it as gradual and those which are clearly described as sudden.

Also, as Hugh Lynn Cayce and Edgar Evans Cayce illustrated so well in their book, *The Outer Limits of Edgar Cayce's Power*, not all of Cayce's predictions were accurate. They cite several possible reasons, which mostly involve the motivations and attunement of not only the channel (Edgar Cayce), but the conductor and the seeker as well. The more sincere, unselfish, and service-oriented each participant was, the more accurate the reading. In addition, the physical environment where the reading was given was important.

1997: The Beginning of Dramatic Change

As Gregg Braden points out in his book *The Isaiah Effect*, there may be something else going on. He notes that "Ancient, as well as modern prophecies suggest that the events of 1997 marked the beginning of a rare period in which we may expect to see some dramatic changes."[1] Cayce's predictions for the beginning of the present millennium seem to have been echoed throughout history within many different cultures. For example, the Mayan calendar tells us that a great cycle of 5,000 years is due to end on December 21, 2012. All previous cycles have ended in catastrophe, including the last one, which was a great worldwide flood occurring about the year 3114 B.C. The Hopi and the Aztecs have similar mythologies. There are Christian groups in this country who believe the "end times" prophecies found in the books of Isaiah, Daniel, and Revelation will either occur soon or are happening right now. Similar concerns were present at the turn of the first millennium A.D. and during other times of crisis in the world.[2] And yet, the world has not ended and the catastrophic earth changes have not occurred. Granted, since September 11, 2001, the potential for catastrophe has become more believable.

A recent scientific article reveals that for the past twenty years, scientists at the Paris Institute of Earth Sciences have been studying variations in the earth's magnetic field through satellite technology. The research team has found evidence that a flip of the magnetic poles may be in the works. A spot in South Africa "has been pointing in the opposite (magnetic) direction from the rest of the Earth's field," and the spot has been growing. According to Gauthier Hulot, the senior author of the article, the last reversal occurred almost 800,000 years ago, and it took several thousand years to complete. Gauthier stressed that "we can't really tell what will happen," but he added, "we're in an unusual situation that might be related to a reversal."[3]

A QUANTUM THEORY OF PROPHECY

In his book, Braden theorizes that prophecy is not an exact science and argues very credibly that it must operate within the laws of physics—specifically, quantum physics. In this view of the universe, the future is made up of probabilities created by choices and actions made in the present. He believes that this has created the seemingly contradictory predictions of many prophets, including Edgar Cayce, as well as Isaiah and St. John. In other words, at the time the prophecy is made, the future appears to be headed in one direction, as in catastrophic disaster. But through the actions, prayers, and changes in consciousness of human beings, another more positive future can also be created. As Braden puts it, " . . . we create the conditions into which we attract future outcomes . . . "[4] The prophets are merely presenting the different options.

Through the discoveries of quantum physics, we know that two atoms, just like two probable futures, can occupy the same space at the same time. With this finding, Braden also raises the provocative possibility that the future you experience may not be the same one I experience. This is reminiscent of John Van Auken's idea that Cayce's "fifth root race" is simply a change in consciousness occurring among certain individuals within the existing population.

The Pulsating Universe and the Isaiah Effect

Braden points out that quantum physics experiments have shown that reality occurs in rapid noncontinuous bursts of light much like frames of a moving picture. We live in a pulsating universe, with space between the pulses. Matter is made of many short bursts. The more bursts, the longer the duration of our experience of reality. Choice points, in which change can occur, are located in the space between the bursts. An example is the still point in the breath between an inhalation and an exhalation. Moving to another outcome may simply be stimulated by the belief that the new reality is already present. Braden calls it "redirecting our focus," an idea much like Cayce's attunement to ideals and seeking at-onement with the Creative Forces.

Braden's theory parallels many of the ideas in the Cayce readings. For example, Cayce often indicated that the future is not set, and that there are certain universal laws that determine what happens to us on both the individual and the group level. Bruce McArthur's popular book on these universal laws, *Your Life*, outlines them very well. Our free will, if we choose to use it, decides not only our own fate, but also the fate of others, since we are all connected.[5] As the Cayce readings tell us, our ultimate goal is to know ourselves to be ourselves and yet one with the whole.[6]

Braden notes that the Essenes believed that "events observed in the world around us mirror the development of beliefs within us."[7] This means that our thoughts and attitudes can actually create or prevent seemingly natural disasters. For example, Cayce noted that human turmoil and strife on earth cause an increase in sunspot activity.[8] Braden believes that the ancient prophets understood this, but that the knowledge was lost because of the restructuring of the Church in A.D. 342. We are just now rediscovering these truths through advancement in our understanding of physics.

As science continues to unveil the holographic nature of the physical world, we can see that each part contains the blueprint for the whole. The "Meditation" chapter in Book I of *A Search for God* states that "So all-inclusive is the physical body that there is nothing in the universe that man can comprehend that does not have its miniature replica within it."[9] At the same time, this means that we are all connected and that prayer can also be a tool to create change in future outcomes. This type of prayer is what Braden calls "the Isaiah Effect," and it is supported by new scientific findings. We participate in the creation of our future whether we want to or not. The challenge is to decide to do so consciously.

In one reading, an individual asked how she should conduct her life in light of Cayce's prophecies for world change. He responded, "*Again* the interpretation of the signs and the omens becomes an individual experience. And each soul—as this entity—then is given the privilege, the opportunity to *live* such an activity in its relationships to its fellow man; filling, fulfilling, and interpreting that which has been indicated, in such measures and such manners as to bring hope and not fear, peace and not hate, that which is *constructive* and *not* destructive, into the lives and minds and hearts of others."[10]

So will the earth changes be gradual or catastrophic? It is up to you—and to me—and the time to decide is now.

29

The Fifth Root Race and 2004

With the storehouse, or record house (where the records are still to be uncovered), there is a chamber or passage from the right forepaw to this entrance of the record chamber, or record tomb. This may not be entered without an understanding, for those that were left as guards may *not* be passed until after a period of their regeneration in the Mount, or the fifth root race begins. 5748-6

For as has been indicated, now, in the next few years [after 1943], there will be many entrances of those who are to prepare the way for the new race, the new experiences of man, that may be a part of those activities in preparation for the day of the Lord. 3514-1

You expect a new root race. What are you doing to prepare for it? You must prepare food for their bodies as well as their minds and their spiritual development! 470-35

With the return then of the priest to the Temple Beautiful . . . leaving first the records of the world from that day until when there is the change in the race. 294-150

According to the Cayce readings we are spiritual beings who have taken on material form. Over millions of years, we became so attached to our earthly portion and detached from our spiritual portion that we began to devolve. Fortunately, the Christ Spirit came into the earth and began a process of rejuvenation that has manifested in leaps of evolution called root races, as discussed in earlier chapters. The human race is currently ending the fourth root race and, according to the readings, will enter the fifth root race soon. It is a process that appears to be gradual and its occurrence is linked to the opening of the Atlantean Halls of Records.

Unfortunately, the readings don't give us many specifics about the nature of the physical change that will manifest in the next root race. However, we do know that it will involve a spiritual transformation and a change in consciousness, and that when it happens some people will not even be aware of it.[1] But the most compelling aspect of this change is that some readings have indicated that it will happen, or at least begin to happen, very soon—perhaps within our lifetime.

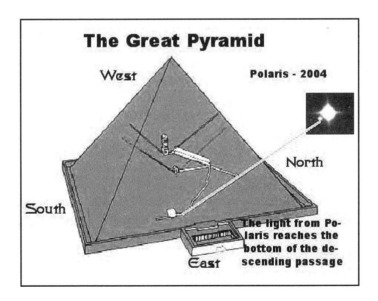

Alignment of Polaris (North Star) with the entrance to the Great Pyramid of Giza in 2004—by G. Little.

POLARIS AND THE GREAT PYRAMID

During the First Annual A.R.E. Members Congress of 1932, Edgar Cayce gave a reading that suggested the next root race would emerge at a time marked by the alignment of the North Star (Polaris) with the entrance to the Great Pyramid. The reading further indicated that these changes were started in 1932, during a time period of difficulty and hardship termed "the Cruciatarian Age." It is at this particular time that " . . . preparations are being made for the beginning of a new sub-race, or a change, which—as indicated from the astronomical or numerical conditions—dates from the latter portion or middle portion of the present fall." The reading further noted that in October of 1932, Jupiter and Uranus would be in a position to bring about "a greater interest in occult or mystic influences."

Cayce was even more specific in the next section, stating,

> At the correct time accurate imaginary lines can be drawn from the opening of the great Pyramid to . . . Polaris . . . and when this change becomes noticeable—as might be calculated from the Pyramid—there will be the beginning of the change in the races. There will come a greater influx of souls from the Atlantean, Lemurian, La, Ur or Da civilizations. 2

This reading becomes especially important given the knowledge that Polaris will be perfectly aligned with the entrance to the Great Pyramid in 2004! At that time, Polaris will shine all the way down the shaft to the Subterranean Passage (also known as the Pit). Even more significant, because the precession of the equinoxes causes the exact position of Polaris in the night sky to change at a rate of one degree every 71.5 years, this means that, in 1932, Polaris was just one degree away from perfect alignment with the entrance.[3,4] This could very well be what Cayce was telling us in this 1932 reading. At that time, Polaris was just getting in position so that it could be seen rising over the edge of the doorway to the Pyramid.

Preparing for the Fifth Root Race

Of course, this doesn't mean that we will wake up on January 1, 2004, and see a new person in the mirror or in the bed lying next to us. As noted in the "Origin of the Races" chapter in this book, Cayce tells us that the change, which could *begin* in 2004, may be so subtle and gradual that some of us will not even be aware that anything has happened.[5] In fact, it appears that we are all very much "works in progress." "Each, in itself, building to itself, through its development known through the ages, as called from the earth plane, that which is manifest upon the earth."[6]

Fortunately (or unfortunately), the readings assure us that our choices and behaviors will influence whether, and how, each of us will enter this new root race. In a 1942 reading related to the purchase of land in the Virginia Beach area for use as a community farm, Cayce stated that the preparation for the future race involves a healthy diet.[7] But he also made clear in many other readings that it very much involves the mind and the will. We have much more control over the final outcome of our development than we realize. The ideals and ideas we choose to focus on are critical to what we will become. "What one thinks continually, they become; what one cherishes in their heart and mind they make a part of the pulsation of their heart, through their own blood cells, and build in their own physical, that which its spirit and soul must feed upon."[8]

Preparing at the Group Level

The Cayce readings tell us that our development as a human race is not only manifested on an individual level, but also at the level of groups and nations. One of the most interesting aspects of the Cayce readings is that they provide information that allows us to view the "personality" of ancient cultures beyond just ruined buildings, burials, and artwork. For example, we are told in one reading that each nation, past and present, has its own spirit and its own downfall. These group characteristics and tendencies influence the development of humanity and therefore the coming of the new root race.[9]

At different times throughout the ages, the readings tell us, some nations "have seen the light" and have tried to establish the highest principles within their laws. America is identified as one of those nations. We are told that America's spirit is "freedom." However, a 1944 reading warned that America's downfall or sin is the tendency to "boast freedom" yet not always practice it. Interestingly, just as the readings state that individuals should strive to know and understand their own motivations and behaviors, it was recommended that all nations, including America, also continually evaluate themselves openly and honestly. "Those nations who have taken those vows that man shall be free should also take those vows 'He shall know the truth and the truth then shall make him free.'"[10]

As has been shown through the various mysteries presented in this book, humans have existed on this planet for millions of years. In the process of moving through each colorful era of history, humanity has both gained and lost in spiritual development. However, as hard as it may be to believe at times, the promise of an imminent fifth root race must mean that we are making progress. In fact, the readings seem to promise continued development into the distant future.

The theory is, man evolved, or evolution, from first cause in creation, and brings forth to meet the needs of the man, the preparation for the needs of man has gone down many, many thousands and millions of years, as is known in this plane, for the needs of man in the hundreds and thousands of years to come.[11]

Endnotes

References for: Chapter 1—Introduction

1. Cayce, E. E., Schwartzer, G., and Richards, D. (1997) *Mysteries of Atlantis Revisited.* New York: St. Martin's Press.
2. Ibid.
3. Reading 364-4.
4. Reading 2665-2.
5. Churchward, J. (1931) *The Lost Continent of Mu.* New York: Ives & Washburn.
6. Hancock, G. (1995) *Fingerprints of the Gods.* London: Crown Publishers.
7. Hancock, G. (2002) *Underworld: The Mysterious Origins of Civilization.* London: Crown Publishers.
8. Collins, A. (2000) *Gateway to Atlantis.* London: Headline Books Publishing.
9. Collins, A. (2001) *From the Ashes of Angels: The Forbidden Legacy of a Fallen Race.* Rochester, VT: Bear & Company.
10. Van Auken, J. and Little, L. (2000) *The Lost Hall of Records: Edgar Cayce's Forgotten Record of Human History in the Ancient Yucatan.* Memphis, TN: Eagle Wing Books, Inc.
11. Little, G., Van Auken, J., and Little, L. (2001) *Mound Builders: Edgar Cayce's Forgotten Record of Ancient America.* Memphis, TN: Eagle Wing Books, Inc.
12. Little, G., Van Auken, J., and Little, L. (2002) *Ancient South America: Recent Evidence Supporting Edgar Cayce's Story of Atlantis and Mu.* Memphis, TN: Eagle Wing Books, Inc.
13. Krajenke, R. (1994) *Edgar Cayce's Story of the Old Testament: From the Birth of Souls to the Death of Moses.* Virginia Beach, VA: A.R.E. Press.

References for: Chapter 2—Origin of the Races

1. Cann, R. et al. (1987) Mitochondrial DNA and human evolution. *Nature,* January.
2. Brunet, M. et al. (2002) *Nature* 418, 145-151.
3. Hammer, M. (1995) A recent common ancestry for human Y chromosomes. *Nature,* 378(6555) 376-8.
4. Thorne, A. (1999). Australia's Oldest Human Remains: Age of the Lake Mungo 3 Skeleton. *Journal of Human Evolution* 36: 591-612.
5. Reading 3003-1.
6. Reading 699-1.

7. Church, W.H. (1995) *Edgar Cayce's Story of the Soul.* Virginia Beach: A.R.E. Press.

8. Reading 281–25.

9. Readings 5748–6, 470–35.

10. Reading 5748–6.

11. Readings 5748–6, 5750–1.

12. Reading 364–10.

13. *Edgar Cayce's Story of the Soul.* op. cit.

14. Van Auken, J. and Little, L. (2000) *The Lost Hall of Records.* Memphis, TN: Eagle Wing Books Inc.

15. Reading 2665–2.

16. Reading 364–10.

17. Reading 364–3.

18. Reading 294–19.

19. Reading 294–150.

20. Reading 364–7.

21. Reading 364–13.

22. Reading 3976–24 and Acts 17:26.

23. Reading 364–13.

24. *Edgar Cayce's Story of the Soul.* op. cit.

25. Reading 1260–1.

26. Reading 364–9.

27. *Lost Hall of Records,* op. cit.

28. Reading 3744–5.

29. Reading 2665–2.

30. Readings 877–10, 5756–11, 364–10.

31. Senut, B. et al. (2001) First hominid from the Miocene (Lukeino formation Kenya) *C.R. Acad. Sci., Paris,* 332, 137–144.

32. Leaky, M. et al. (2001) New hominin genus from eastern Africa shows diverse middle Pliocene lineages. *Nature,* 410, 433–440.

33. Reading 3188–1.

34. Reading 1602–3.

35. Reading 5749–14.

36. Reading 349–4.

References—Chapter 3: Lilith and Amilius

1. Kramer, S. (1938) Gilgamesh and the Huluppu-Tree: A reconstructed Sumerian text. *Assyriological Studies of the Oriental Institute of the University of Chicago, 10.*

2. Stern, D. and Mirsky, M. J. (1990) *Rabbinic Fantasies: Imaginative Narratives from Classical Hebrew Literature.* Philadelphia: Jewish Publication Society.

3. The *Targum Yerushalmi* is an Aramaic version of the Torah. The manuscripts of the Targums date from the eleventh through the thirteenth centuries.

4. The ideas in this section may be found throughout Edgar Cayce's readings, but especially in the 364 series in response to Cayce's request for information on Atlantis.

5. Patanjali, *Yoga Sutra* (ca. 300–400–B.C.).

6. Ibid. *Yoga Sutra, III. Vibhuti-Pada* ("Chapter on Powers").

References for: Chapter 4—Eve and Adam

1. Reading 900–181.

2. Zodhiates, S., Th.D. (1990) *The Hebrew-Greek Key Study Bible.* AMG Publishers.

3. Readings 900–227, 364–9, 364–13.

4. Reading 2072–10.

5. Reading 281–33.

6. Reading 815–7.

7. Reading 3653–1.

References for: Chapter 5—Noah's Flood

1. Readings 2627–1, 3653–1, 2425–1, 2624–1.

2. Reading 2547–1.

3. Reading 364–6.

4. Reading 470–22.

5. Readings 364–4, 288–1.

6. Firestone, R. and Topping, W. (2001) Terrestrial Evidence of a Nuclear Catastrophe in Paleo–Indian Times, *The Mammoth Trumpet*, March.

7. Jakeman, M. (1963) The Flood Story of Genesis. In Ross T. Christensen (Ed.) *Progress in Archaeology: An Anthology.* Provo, Utah: Brigham Young University, pp. 11–16.

8. Ryan, W. and Pitman, W. (1999) *Noah's Flood: The New Scientific Discoveries About the Event That Changed History.* New York: Simon & Schuster.

9. Aksu, A. et al. (2002) Persistent Holocene Outflow from the Black Sea to the Eastern Mediterranean Contradicts Noah's Flood Hypothesis, *GSA Today,* May.

10. Brown, Irene (2002) Satellite Combs Mountain for Noah's Ark. *Discovery News,* Sept. 12.

11. Reading 2627–1.

12. Reading 364–10.

13. Reading 294–150.

14. Krajenke, R. (1973) *Edgar Cayce's Story of the Old Testament: From the Birth of Souls to the Death of Moses.* Virginia Beach: A.R.E. Press.

15. Van Auken, J. (2001) Holy wars. *Living in the Light* newsletter, 31, October.

16. Reading 1602–3.

17. Reading 3653–1.

References for: Chapter 6—Genetics Research

1. Little, G. L., Van Auken, J., and Little, L. (2002) *Ancient South America: Recent Evidence Supporting Edgar Cayce's Story of Atlantis and Mu.* Memphis, TN: Eagle Wing Books, Inc.

2. Reading 364–4.

3. Reading 1387–1.

4. Reading 364–17.

5. Reading 2665–2.

6. Readings 5750–1, 364 series, and 5748 series.

7. Feder, K. (1990; 1996) *Frauds, Myths, and Mysteries: Science and Pseudoscience in Archaeology, Mountain View,* CA: Mayfield Publishing Company.

8. Malhi, R. et al. (2002) The structure of diversity within New World mitochondrial DNA haplogroups: Implications for the prehistory of North America. *American Journal of Human Genetics,* 70.

9. Milnor, P. and Little, G. (2000) *It Can Break Your Heart.* Memphis, TN: Eagle Wing Books.

10. Little, G. L., Van Auken, J., and Little, L. (2001) *Mound Builders: Edgar Cayce's Forgotten Record of Ancient America.* Memphis, TN: Eagle Wing Books, Inc.

11. Brunet, M. et al. (2002) *Nature* 418, 145–151.

12. *Ancient South America,* op. cit.

13. *Mound Builders*, op. cit.

14. Van Auken, J. and Little, L. (2001) *The Lost Hall of Records*. Memphis, TN: Eagle Wing Books, Inc.

15. *Ancient South America*, op. cit.

16. Izaguirre, N. and Rua, C. (1999) An mtDNA analysis in ancient Basque populations: Implications for haplogroup V as a marker for a major Paleolithic expansion from southwestern Europe. *American Journal of Human Genetics*, 65.

17. *American Journal of Human Genetics*, 70, op. cit.

18. *Ancient South America*, op. cit.

19. Readings 816-3 and 851-2.

20. Hurse, M. et al. (2002) Y chromosomal evidence for the origins of the Oceanic-speaking peoples. *Genetics*, 160.

References for: Chapter 7—The Search for the Halls of Records

1. Readings 2329-3, 378-16.

2. Readings 440-5, 2012-1.

3. Reading 378-16.

4. Cayce, E., Schwartzer, G., and Richards, D. (1997) *Mysteries of Atlantis Revisited*. New York: St. Martin's Press.

5. Hancock, G. and Bauval, R. (1996) *The Message of the Sphinx: A Quest for the Hidden Legacy of Mankind*. New York: Crown Publishers.

6. Ibid.

7. Little, L. and Little, G. (Nov/Dec 2002) *Ancient Mysteries Newsletter*. Virginia Beach, VA: Association for Research and Enlightenment, Inc.

8. Reading 440-5.

9. Van Auken, J. and Little, L (2000) *The Lost Hall of Records: Edgar Cayce's Forgotten Record of Human History in the Ancient Yucatan*. Memphis, TN: Eagle Wing Books, Inc.

10. Houston, S. et al. (2000) In the Land of the Turtle Lords: Archaeological Investigations at Piedras Negras, Guatemala, 2000. *Mexicon*, XXII, pp. 97–110.

11. McGahan, J. (2003) Maya Sites Face Flooding. *Archaeology Magazine Online*, 02/19/03.

12. Reading 958-3.

13. Joseph, F. (Fall 1996) Project Alta: Search and Discovery in the Bahamas.

Ancient American Magazine, Vol. 3, No. 23. pp. 2–4.

14. Harrison, W. (1971) Atlantis Undiscovered – Bimini, Bahamas. *Nature*, 230, pp. 287–289.

15. Hanley, Joan (1997) Bimini Road: Getting to the Core of the Matter. *Ancient American*, Vol. 3, No. 19/20, pp. 38–39.

16. *Mysteries of Atlantis Revisited*, op. cit.

17. Reading 364-3.

18. Cawthorne, A. (2001) Explorers Comb Cuban Seas for Treasure, Mysteries. *Reuters News Service*, May 14.

19. Little, L. and Little, G. (2002) Ancient Mysteries and Modern Discoveries: Report on the Annual Egypt and Ancient Civilizations Conference. *Ancient Mysteries Newsletter*, Nov/Dec.

20. Reading 996-12.

References for: Chapter 8—
Honeycombed Mountains and Perpetual Fires

1. Reading 5748-6.

2. Hancock, G. and Bauval, R. (1996) *The Message of the Sphinx: A Quest for the Hidden Legacy of Mankind*. New York: Crown Publishers.

3. Reading 294-150.

4. Reading 294-149.

5. Reading 294-150.

6. Reading 2923-3.

7. Reading 416-1.

8. Reading 816-3.

9. Reading 559-7.

10. Reading 294-150.

11. Reading 294-151.

12. Parsons, Geoffrey (1931) *The Stream of History*. New York: Charles Scribner's Sons.

13. Westcott, W. Rosicrucian Thoughts on the Ever-Burning Lamps of the Ancients. VIII, *Frater Roseae Crusis*. Web site: www.levity.com/alchemy/westcott.

14. Lhote, H. (1977) When the Sahara was green. In *The World's Last Mysteries*. Pleasantville, New York: The Reader's Digest Association, Inc.

15. de Prorok, B. (1926) *Digging for Lost African Gods.* New York: G. P. Putnam and Sons.
16. Reading 364–13.
17. Web site: volcano.und.nodak.edu/vwdocs/volc_images/africa/ fantale.html.
18. Arkell, A.J. 1955. *A History of the Sudan from the Earliest Times to 1821.* London.
19. Doresse, J. (1959) *Ethiopia.* New York: Frederick Ungar Publishing Co.
20. Gates, Jr., H. (1999) *Wonders of the African World.* New York: Alfred A. Knopf, p. 99.
21. Reading 364–13.
22. Reading 294–150.
23. Reading 281–10.
24. Reading 294–151.
25. *ABC News Online,* May 8 2002. Web site: www.abc.net.au/science/news/ scitech/SciTechRepublish_550172.htm.
26. Burstein, S. (1998) *Ancient African Civilizations: Kush and Axum.* Princeton, NJ: Markus Wiener Publishers.
27. Slayman, A. (1998) Neolithic skywatchers. *Archaeology Magazine Online News.* Web site: www.archaeology.org/online/news/nubia.html.
28. *Wonders of the African World,* op. cit.
29. Kendall, Timothy. *The Gebel Barkal Temples 1989-90: A Progress Report on the Work of the Museum of Fine Arts, Boston, Sudan Mission.* Geneva: 7th International Conference for Nubian Studies, 3–8 Sept., 1990.

References for: Chapter 9—The Pyramids: Where Was the First?

1. Schoch. R. M. (2003) *Voyages of the Pyramid Builders.* NY: Tarcher.
2. Sharer, R. (1994) *The Ancient Maya.* Stanford, CA: Stanford University Press.
3. Saunders, J. et al. (1997) A mound complex in Louisiana at 5400–5000 years before present. *Science,* 277, 1796.
4. Gibson, J. (1983) *Poverty Point, Baton Rouge: Louisiana Archaeological Survey and Antiquities Commission Anthropological Study No. 7.*
5. Reading 5750–1.
6. Readings 993–3 and 2124–4.
7. Reading 364–12.

8. Reading 2121–2.

9. Plato's Dialogues, *Critias and Timaeus*.

10. Casson, L. (1965) *Ancient Egypt*. NY: Time–Life.

11. Cayce, E. E., Schwartzer, G. C., and Richards, D. G. (1997) *Mysteries of Atlantis Revisited*. NY: St. Martins Paperback, p. 146.

12. *Discovery News*, 12/04/02.

13. Kramer, S. N. (1967) *Cradle of Civilization*. NY: Time–Life.

14. Rohl, D. (1998) *Legend: The Genesis of Civilization*. London: Century, Random House.

15. Genesis 10:10, Genesis 11

16. Genesis 11.

17. *BBCNews Online*. April 29, 2003.

18. Jacobs, J. A. (2000) Early monumental architecture on the Peruvian coast: Evidence of socio–political organization and the variation in its interpretation. Available online at: www.jqjacobs.net

19. Little, G. L., Van Auken, J., and Little, L. (2002) *Ancient South America: Recent Evidence Supporting Edgar Cayce's Story of Atlantis and Mu*. Memphis, TN: Eagle Wing Books, Inc.

20. *The Times of India* (May 20, 2001) Harappan–like ruins discovered in Gulf of Cambay.

21. Mohapatra, G. P., and M. H. Prasad (1999) Shoreline changes and their impact on the archaeological structures at Mahabalipuram. *Gondwana Geological Magazine*, 4, 225–233.

22. Gangopadhyay, Uttara (May 2, 2003) India's underwater heritage. *Asia Times Online*.

23. The premiere web site for online information on the Harappan culture is: www.harappa.com

24. Pyramid built 5000 years ago found in Inner Mongolia. *People's Daily Online*, July 6, 2001.

25. Reading 3420–1.

26. Reading 3102–2.

27. Reading 1604–1.

28. Reading 1486–1.

29. Reading 1143–2.

30. Reading 906–3.

31. Little, G. L., Van Auken, J., and Little, L. (2001) *Mound Builders: Edgar Cayce's*

Forgotten Record of Ancient America. Memphis: Eagle Wing Books, Inc.

References for: Chapter 10—
The Pyramids: How Were the Stones Moved?

1. Reading 5750-1.
2. Reading 5748-6.
3. Reading 262-39.
4. Cayce, E.E. (1968) *Edgar Cayce on Atlantis.* New York: Warner Books, Inc.
5. Cayce, E.E., Schwartzer, G., and Richards, D. (1997) *Mysteries of Atlantis Revisited.* New York: St. Martins Paperbacks.
6. A 2003 recount of the stones of the Great Pyramid showed that it is constructed of one million stones rather than the 2.3 million figure typically cited. *Ancient Mysteries* newsletter, February 2003.
7. Dr. Clemmons' web site contains a summary of her findings: www.fdsmail.com/archeologee.
8. Little, G. L., Van Auken, J., and Little, L. (2002) *Ancient South America: Recent Evidence Supporting Edgar Cayce's Story of Atlantis and Mu.* Memphis, TN: Eagle Wing Books, Inc.

References for: Chapter 11—The Pyramids: Who Built Teotihuacán?

1. Ferguson, W., Rohn, A., and Royce, J. (1990) *Mesoamerica's Ancient Cities.* Niwot, Colorado: University Press of Colorado.
2. (2002) Was Maya Pyramid Designed to Chirp Like a Bird? *National Geographic Today,* 12/06.
3. Manzanilla, L., Lopez, C., and Freter, A. (1996) Dating results from excavations in quarry tunnels behind the pyramid of the sun at Teotihuacán. *Ancient Mesoamerica,* 7, 245–266.
4. (2001) Excavations challenge views of Maya development in Yucatan. *National Geographic News,* May 17.
5. Freidel, D., Schele, L., and Parker, J. (1995) *Maya Cosmos.* New York: William Morrow.
6. Reading 5750-1.
7. Sorenson, J. (1985) *An Ancient American Setting for the Book of Mormon.* Salt Lake City, Utah: Deseret Book Company.
8. Edgar Cayce Readings CD-ROM, Letter to Mrs. (1319).
9. Reading 1438-1.

References for: Chapter 12—
The Great Wall of Peru and the Mysterious Ohums:

1. Reading 364-4.
2. Church, W. H. (1989). *Edgar Cayce's Story of the Soul*. Virginia Beach, VA: A.R.E. Press.
3. Cayce, E. E. (1968) *Edgar Cayce on Atlantis*. Virginia Beach, VA: A.R.E. Press.
4. Little, G. L., Van Auken, J., and Little, L. (2002) *Ancient South America: Recent Evidence Supporting Edgar Cayce's Story of Atlantis and Mu*. Memphis, TN: Eagle Wing Books, Inc.
5. *Smithsonian Institution Annual Report* (1932) Washington, D.C.: U.S. Government Printing Office.
6. *Edgar Cayce's Story of the Soul*, op. cit., pp. 184-188.
7. *Ancient South America*, op. cit., p. 88.
8. *Smithsonian Institution Annual Report*, op. cit., p. 461.
9. Corliss, W. R. (1978) *Ancient Man*. Glen Arm, MD: Sourcebook Project, pp. 92-96.
10. *Edgar Cayce's Story of the Soul*, op. cit.

References for: Chapter 13—Cayce's Ancient India

1. (2002) 7500 BC lost river civilization discovered off India's coast. *The Times of India Online*. January 16.
2. Rao, Rajyasri (2001) Indian seabed hides ancient remains. *BBC News Online Network*, May 22.
3. (1999) 'Earliest writing' found. *BBC News Online Network*, May 4.
4. Reading 5249-1.
5. Readings 1391-1, 1483-1, 1210-1.
6. Church, W. H. (1995) *The Lives of Edgar Cayce*. Virginia Beach, VA: A.R.E. Press.
7. Reading 364-13.
8. Hancock, Graham (2002) *Underworld: The Mysterious Origins of Civilization*. New York: Crown Publishers.
9. Reading 900-277.
10. Reading 294-150.
11. Reading 984-1.
12. Reading 987-2.

13. Readings 294-147, 2420-1.

14. Reading 866-1.

15. (2002) India's miracle river. *BBC News Online Network*, June 29.

16. Rajaram, N. S. (2001) DNA and the human past. *The Hindu*, August 07.

17. Raman, S. R. (2003) Of lasting genes and lost cities of Tamil Nadu. *Hindustan Times.com*, January 05.

18. Reading 866-1.

19. Reading 812-1.

References for: Chapter 14—America's Mound Builders

1. Cayce, E.E., Schwartzer, G., and Richards, D. (1997) *Mysteries of Atlantis Revisited.* New York: St. Martins Paperbacks.

2. Little, G. L., Van Auken, J., and Little, L. (2001) *Mound Builders: Edgar Cayce's Forgotten Record of Ancient America.* Memphis: Eagle Wing Books, Inc.

3. Folsom, F., and Folsom, M. (1993) *America's Ancient Treasures.* Albuquerque: University of New Mexico Press.

4. National Geographic Society & Dallas Museum of Natural History Joint Press Release. (February 10, 1997) Chilean site verified as earliest habitation of Americas: Findings show Monte Verde dates back 12,000 years.

5. Reading 5750-1.

6. Reading 3528-1.

7. Snow, D. (1976) *The Archaeology of North America.* London: Thames and Hudson.

8. Saunders, J. W., Jones, R., Moorhead, K., and Davis, B. (1998) Watson Brake objects: An unusual archaic artifact type from Northeast Louisiana and Southwest Mississippi. *Southeastern Archaeology*, 17, 72-79.

9. *The Jewish Encyclopedia* (1905) London: Funk and Wagnalls.

References for: Chapter 15—Egyptians in Ancient America

1. Reading 3528-1.

2. Reading 500-1.

3. Reading 1434-1.

4. Reading 1144-2.

5. Williamson, R. A. (Ed.) (1981) *Archaeoastronomy in the Americas.* College Park,

MD: The Center for Archaeoastronomy.

6. McGlone, B., Leonard, P., and Barker, T. (1999) *Archaeoastronomy of Southeast Colorado and the Oklahoma Panhandle.* Kamas, UT: Mithras, Inc.

7. Little, G. L., Van Auken, J., and Little, L. (2001) *Mound Builders: Edgar Cayce's Forgotten Record of Ancient America.* Memphis, TN: Eagle Wing Books, Inc.

8. Reading 1473-1.

References for: Chapter 16—Odin

1. Sturluson, S. (1908) The *Elder* or *Poetic Edda.* London: Viking Club.

2. Reading 1468-6.

3. Reading 441-1.

4. Reading 2124-3.

5. Reading 3479-2.

6. Reading 364-13.

References for: Chapter 17—Tower of Babel: An Atlantean Legend?

1. Jakeman, M. W. (1963) The Flood Story of Genesis. In Ross T. Christensen (Ed.) *Progress in Archaeology: An Anthology.* Provo, Utah: Brigham Young University, pp. 11-16.

2. Cottrell, L. (1964) *The Concise Encyclopedia of Archaeology.* New York: Hawthorn Books, Inc.

3. (2003) History in harm's way. *Sidney Morning Herald* March 29.

4. *The Concise Encyclopedia of Archaeology,* op. cit.

5. Ibid.

6. *The Jewish Encyclopedia,* 1905.

7. Rappoport, A. (1928) *Myth and Legend of Ancient Israel, Volume 1.* London: Gresham Publishing Company, p. 235.

8. *The Jewish Encyclopedia,* 1905.

9. Ibid.

10. Reading 5750-1.

11. Sorenson, J. (1985) *An Ancient American Setting for the Book of Mormon.* Salt Lake City, Utah: Deseret Book Company.

12. Krajenke, R. (1994) *Edgar Cayce's Story of the Old Testament: From the Birth of Souls to the Death of Moses.* Virginia Beach, VA: A.R.E. Press.

13. *The Jewish Encyclopedia,* 1905.

14. Graves, R. and Patai, R. (1983) *Hebrew Myths: The Book of Genesis*. New York: Greenwich House.

15. Reading 440-5.

16. *Hebrew Myths*, op. cit.

17. Reading 262-099.

18. Reading 262-96.

References for: Chapter 18—Sodom and Gomorrah

1. Rappoport, A. (1928) *Myth and Legend of Ancient Israel Volume 1*. London: Gresham Publishing Company, p. 264.

2. Ibid.

3. Albright, W.F. (1948) Exploring in Sinai with the University of California Africa expedition, *Bulletin of the American Schools of Oriental Research* 109 (1948): 1-20.

4. Schaub, R. and Rast, W. (1989) *Bab edh-Dhra': Excavations in the Cemetery Directed by Paul Lapp: Reports of the Expedition to the Dead Sea Plains—REDSP 1*. Eisenbrauns.

5. Price, R. (1997) *The Stones Cry Out*. Eugene, OR: Harvest House Publishers.

6. Childress, D. (2000) *Technologies of the Gods: The Incredible Sciences of the Ancients*. Steele, IL: Adventures Unlimited Press.

7. Philby, J. St. J. B. (1933) *The Empty Quarter*. New York: Henry Holt.

8. Shoemaker, E. and Wynn, J. (1995) Geology of the Wabar Meteorite Craters, Saudi Arabia. U. S. Geological Survey, Reston, VA.

9. Koeberl, C. (2000) Confirmation of a Meteoritic Component in Libyan Desert Glass From Osmium Isotope Data. Institute of Geochemistry, University of Vienna, Althanstrasse 14, A-1090 Vienna, Austria.

10. Reading 262-28.

11. Krajenke, R. (1994) *Edgar Cayce's Story of the Old Testament: From the Birth of Souls to the Death of Moses*. Virginia Beach, VA: A.R.E. Press.

12. Reading 294-136.

13. Reading 1598-2.

14. Reading 3976-8.

References for: Chapter 19—The Mysterious Oracle Stones

1. *The Jewish Encyclopedia*, 1905.

2. Readings 355-1, 294-142.

3. Reading 261-015.

4. *The Jewish Encyclopedia*, 1905.

5. Reading 440-11.

6. Cook, F (1905) *The Bible Commentary: Book of Exodus, 28.* New York: Charles Scribner's Sons.

7. *The Jewish Encyclopedia*, 1905, Vol. XI, p. 385.

8. Ibid.

9. Reading 2072-10.

10. Reading 5750-1.

11. Reading 440-5.

12. *The Bible Commentary*, op. cit.

13. Rappoport, A. (1928) *Myth and Legend of Ancient Israel, Volume II.* London: Gresham Publishing Company.

14. *The Jewish Encyclopedia*, 1905.

15. Reading 5294-1.

16. Van Auken, J. and Little, L. (2000) *The Lost Hall of Records: Edgar Cayce's Forgotten Record of Human History in the Ancient Yucatan.* Memphis, TN: Eagle Wing Books, Inc.

17. Online Mineral Gallery. See web site: www.minerals.net/mineral, copyright Hershel Friedman, 1997-1999.

18. *The Bible Commentary*, op. cit.

19. Reading 261-15.

References for: Chapter 20—The Parting of the Red Sea

1. Moller, L. (2000) *The Exodus case.* Stockholm, Sweden: Scandinavia Publishing House.

2. *Exodus Discovered.* (Videotape; no date given) Cornersville, TN: Wyatt Archaeological Research *Surprising Discoveries 2.* (Videotape; no date given) Adelaide, Australia: J. Gray.

3. Humphreys, C. (2003) *The Miracles of Exodus: A Scientist's Discovery of the Extraordinary Natural Causes of the Biblical Stories.* San Francisco: Harper.

References for: Chapter 21—Immaculate Conception

1. Ruggles, R. (1999) *Apparition Shrines: Places of Pilgrimage and Prayer.*

Boston: Pauline Books and Media.

2. Ibid.
3. Cranston, R. (1955) *The Miracle of Lourdes.* New York: McGraw–Hill.
4. *Apparition Shrines: Places of Pilgrimage and Prayer,* op. cit.
5. Harris, R. (1999) *Lourdes: Body and Spirit in the Secular Age.* New York: Viking Penguin.
6. West, D. (1957) *Eleven Lourdes Miracles.* New York: Helix Press.
7. Rogo, D.S. (1983) *Miracles: A Parascientific Inquiry into Wondrous Phenomena.* Chicago: Contemporary Books, Inc.
8. *Apparition Shrines: Places of Pilgrimage and Prayer,* op. cit.
9. *Miracles: A Parascientific Inquiry into Wondrous Phenomena,* op. cit.
10. *Lourdes: Body and Spirit in the Secular Age,* op. cit.
11. Op. cit., p. 25.
12. Op. cit., p. 38.
13. *Apparition Shrines: Places of Pilgrimage and Prayer,* op. cit.
14. Reading 5749-8.
15. Reading 2067-11.
16. Reading 5749-7.
17. Reading 5749-8.
18. Readings 364-3, 364-5, 364-7.
19. Reading 2072-3.
20. Reading 5749-7.
21. Readings 5749-7, 2072-4.
22. Brown, R. (1951) *The Life of Mary As Seen By The Mystics.* Rockford, IL: Tan Books and Publishers, Inc.
23. Finegan, J. (1992) *The Archaeology of The New Testament.* Princeton, NJ: Princeton University Press.
24. Reading 5749-8.
25. Ibid.

References for: Chapter 22—Wise Men from the East
1. Reading 5749-7.
2. Reading 2067-7.
3. Ibid.

4. Asimov, I. (1969) *Asimov's Guide to the Bible: The New Testament.* New York: Avon Books.

5. Reading 2982–4.

6. *The Jewish Encyclopedia*, 1905, Vol.VIII, p. 255.

7. Ibid.

8. Readings 256–1, 1908–1.

9. Reading 5749–7.

10. Reading 1010–17.

11. Reading 1472–3.

12. Reading 5749–2.

13. Reading 2067–1.

14. Kirkpatrick, S. (2000) *Edgar Cayce: An American Prophet.* New York: Riverhead Books.

15. Reading 5749–7.

16. Fillmore, C. (1931) *The Metaphysical Bible Dictionary.* Unity Village, MO: Unity Books, p. 677.

17. Delaney, J. (1983) *The Pocket Dictionary of Saints.* New York: Doubleday.

References for: Chapter 23—Resurrection and Regeneration

1. Reading 1152–1.

2. *The Jewish Encyclopedia*, 1905.

3. *Catechism of the Catholic Church: for the United States of America* (1994) United Catholic Conference, Inc. Libreria Editrice Vaticana, p. 260.

4. Reading 2533–4.

5. Reading 294–150.

6. Graves, R. and Patai, R. (1983) *Hebrew Myths: The Book of Genesis.* New York: Greenwich House.

7. Reading 5023–2.

8. *Catechism of the Catholic Church*, op cit., p. 252.

9. Cruz, J. (1977) *The Incorruptibles.* Rockford, IL: Tan Books and Publishers, Inc.

10. Reading 2533–4.

11. Reading 294–152.

12. Reading 2156–2.

References for: Chapter 24—Speaking with Tongues of Fire

1. Reading 294-192.
2. (1976) *Early Christian Epoch: The Edgar Cayce Readings (Library Series Volume 6)*. Virginia Beach, VA: A.R.E. Press.
3. Furst, J. (1976) *Edgar Cayce's Story of Jesus*. New York: Berkley Books.
4. Reading 294-192.
5. Guinness, A. (1988) *Mysteries of the Bible*. The Reader's Digest, Inc.
6. Reading 792-2.
7. Reading 2425-1.
8. Ibid.
9. *The New Catholic Encyclopedia*, 1967.
10. Cook, F. (1905) *The Bible Commentary: Acts of the Apostles: 2*. New York: Charles Scribner's Sons, p. 362.
11. *The New Catholic Encyclopedia*, 1967.
12. Finegan, J. (1992) *The Archaeology of The New Testament*. Princeton, NJ: Princeton University Press.
13. Read, A. (1970) *Edgar Cayce on Jesus and His Church*. New York: Paperbook Library.
14. Reading 262-87.

References for: Chapter 25—El Camino de Santiago

1. Westwood, J. (1987) *The Atlas of Mysterious Places*. New York: Weidenfeld & Nicolson.
2. MacLaine, S. (2000) *The Camino: A Journey of the Spirit*. New York: Pocket Books.
3. (2000) *Santiago History and Legends*. See web site: www.red2000.com/spain/santiago/history.html.
4. Reading 2390-3.
5. Reading 1158-5.
6. Reading 2390-3.
7. *Santiago History and Legends*, op. cit.
8. Freidel, D., Schele, L., and Parker, J. (1995) *Maya Cosmos*. New York: William Morrow.
9. (2002) Medieval footpath under the stars of the Milky Way. *Telegraph Online Newspaper*, April 1.

10. (2003) The Oldest Burial Object. *Guardian, U.K.*, January 9.
11. Readings 815–2, 315–4.
12. Medieval footpath under the stars of the Milky Way, op. cit.
13. Ibid.
14. Reading 5750–1.
15. *Maya Cosmos*, op. cit.

References for: Chapter 26—Paradise: Where and When?
1. Reading 262–92.
2. Reading 5036–1.
3. Reading 2505–1.
4. Reading 262–29.
5. Reading 900–16.
6. Reading 262–77.
7. Reading 262–87.
8. Reading 281–37.
9. Reading 262–88.

References for: Chapter 27—The Mystery of the Second Coming
1. Reading 5749–5.
2. Ibid.
3. Reading 262–58.
4. Reading 5749–5.
5. Ibid.
6. Reading 262–49.
7. Reading 5749–5.
8. Reading 262–58.

References for: Chapter 28—
Quantum Physics and the Science of Prophecy
1. Braden, G. (2000) *The Isaiah Effect: Decoding the Lost Science of Prayer and Prophecy*. New York: Three Rivers Press, p. 16.
2. Van Auken, J. (2001) *The End Times: Prophecies of Coming Changes*. New York: New American Library.

3. Gauthier, H. et al. (2002) Small-scale structure of the geodynamo inferred from Oersted and Magsat satellite data, *Nature* 416, 620–623 (11 April).

4. *The Isaiah Effect*, op. cit., p. 24.

5. McArthur, B. (1993) *Your Life: Why It Is The Way It Is and What You Can Do About It*. Virginia Beach. VA: A.R.E. Press.

6. Reading 281-37.

7. *The Isaiah Effect*, op. cit., p. 22.

8. Reading 5757-1.

9. A.R.E (1942) *A Search for God: Book I*. Virginia Beach, VA: A.R.E. Press, p. 7.

10. Reading 1602-5.

References for: Chapter 29 – Fifth Root Race and 2004

1. Reading 1602-3.

2. Reading 5748-6.

3. Zajaz, J. (2001) Inside the Great Pyramid of Giza: As Above, So Below. Online Newsletter (Ed.) Arvid Luneng, October 12. See web site: http://home.online.no/~luneng/nrthstr.htm.

4. Spence, K. (2000) Ancient Egyptian chronology and the astronomical orientation of pyramids. *Nature*, 408, 320–324.

5. Reading 1602-3.

6. Reading 3744-5.

7. Reading 470-35.

8. Reading 3744-5.

9. Reading 3976-29.

10. Ibid.

11. Reading 3744-5.

Index

247

A.R.E. PRESS

The A.R.E. Press publishes books, videos, and audiotapes meant to improve the quality of our readers' lives—personally, professionally, and spiritually. We hope our products support your endeavors to realize your career potential, to enhance your relationships, to improve your health, and to encourage you to make the changes necessary to live a loving, joyful, and fulfilling life.

For more information or to receive a free catalog, call:

1–800–723–1112

Or write:

A.R.E. Press
215 67th Street
Virginia Beach, VA 23451–2061

DISCOVER HOW THE EDGAR CAYCE MATERIAL CAN HELP YOU!

The Association for Research and Enlightenment, Inc. (A.R.E.®), was founded in 1931 by Edgar Cayce. Its international headquarters are in Virginia Beach, Virginia, where thousands of visitors come year-round. Many more are helped and inspired by A.R.E's local activities in their own hometowns or by contact via mail (and now the Internet!) with A.R.E. headquarters.

People from all walks of life, all around the world, have discovered meaningful and life-transforming insights in the A.R.E. programs and materials, which focus on such areas as personal spirituality, holistic health, dreams, family life, finding your best vocation, reincarnation, ESP, meditation, and soul growth in small-group settings. Call us today at our toll-free number:

1-800-333-4499

or

Explore our electronic visitors center on the
Internet: **http://www.edgarcayce.org.**

We'll be happy to tell you more about how the work of the A.R.E. can help you!

A.R.E.
215 67th Street
Virginia Beach, VA 23451-2061